Conjure Times

Other Walker & Company books by Jim Haskins

From Afar to Zulu: A Dictionary of African Tribes

Spike Lee: By Any Means Necessary

Conjure

Black Magicians

Walker & Company   New York

Times

in America

Jim Haskins and Kathleen Benson

First published in the United States of America in 2001 by
Walker Publishing Company, Inc.

Published simultaneously in Canada by Fitzhenry and Whiteside,
Markham, Ontario L3R 4T8

Library of Congress Cataloging-in-Publication Data

Haskins, James, 1941–
Conjure times : black magicians in America / Jim Haskins and
Kathleen Benson.
p. cm.
ISBN 0-8027-8762-2 (hc) — ISBN 0-8027-8763-0
1. African American magicians—Biography—Juvenile literature.
[1. Magicians. 2. African Americans—Biography.]
I. Benson, Kathleen. II. Title.

GV1545.A2 H37 2001
793.8'092'396073—dc21
[B] 00-069335

Book design by Ellen Cipriano

Printed in the United States of America

2 4 6 8 10 9 7 5 3 1

To Margaret Emily

Contents

Acknowledgments

The authors are grateful to Jim Magus, author of *Magical Heroes: The Lives and Legends of Great African American Magicians*. Privately published in 1995 in a limited run of 600 copies, the book is the result of twenty years of investigating and collecting memorabilia on these undeservedly obscure people who brought wonder, excitement, and laughs to audiences black and white. The authors are also indebted to the following people who provided information on African-American magicians for this book and provided leads to other sources of information: Charles Greene, magician extraordinaire; Hal Hale, librarian at the Magic Castle in Los Angeles; Lemont Haskins, also known as Magic Monty; Gary Hunt, co-editor of *Magical Past-Times: The On-Line Journal of Magic History*; and Dave Price. Also, Debbie Cox of the Metropolitan Government Archives, Public Library of Nashville and Davidson County, Tennessee; Henry G. Fulmer, Manuscripts Librarian, University of South Carolina; and Ann Allen Shockley, Associate Librarian for Special Collections and University Archivist, Fisk University Library. A special thank-you to Patricia Allen for her research work.

Conjure Times

Introduction

Black Conjurers in Time

Charles Greene III unwinds a long string of dental floss from its white plastic case and holds it up for his audience to see. Standing behind a carpeted lectern attached to the Johnson & Johnson display at a dental trade show at the Jacob K. Javits convention center in New York City, he flashes a big smile at the dozen or so people who have stopped to watch him perform his twice-hourly routine on behalf of his corporate client. Holding the string of floss aloft, he proceeds to cut half of it into small pieces. He crushes the sticky material into a tight wad and sticks it to the remaining piece of string, then asks a member of his audience to pull one end. Miraculously, the floss becomes one piece again. His audience marvels. Some have been back to watch him two or three times. Greene performs card tricks, rope tricks, and assorted other illusions, all the while cleverly relating them to the corporation he is representing, the pharmaceutical company

Famous black photographer James VanDerZee documented
this black escape artist in 1924, two years before the death
of Harry Houdini, the famous white "self-liberator."
Unfortunately, the black man is otherwise unidentified.

Photograph by James VanDerZee, 1924

Copyright (c) Donna Mussenden VanDerZee

Johnson & Johnson. He specializes in corporate trade-show magic and is the only African-American magician currently pursuing that particular specialty. As a black magician, however, he is part of a long continuum that goes back to the early days of this nation.

Greene is carrying on a tradition of magic as entertainment that has existed since ancient times and the early days of America. A French conjurer named Jean Eugène Robert Houdin (1805–1871) is regarded as the founder of modern magic. Indeed, the greatest magician of all time, Harry Houdini, took his stage name from that of the French conjurer.

Magic as entertainment has little relationship to so-called black magic or witchcraft, an activity in which the practitioners claim to be able to affect people's lives for good or ill and which has strong associations with the Devil and the supernatural. Nor is it used to refer to religious or spiritual beliefs and practices. The term *magicians* is used in this book to describe entertainers with skill in various tricks. They include ventriloquism (the ability to "throw" one's voice, so that it appears to emanate from a different person, animal, or thing), sleight-of-hand (causing the audience to look elsewhere so they miss how the performer produces a rabbit from a hat, or a cage of live doves from a silk scarf), mind-reading (the ability to tell what someone else is thinking), levitation (the ability to raise oneself or another person into the air), and similar illusions that the average onlooker cannot explain.

All great magicians also have another skill—an understanding of psychology. Most magic depends on using the power of suggestion to change the direction of the audience's thought processes, so that the mind thinks the eye sees something when it does not.

Charles Greene has made a specialty of trade-show magic.
He uses illusions and sleight-of-hand to educate people
about the qualities of the products he represents. Here, he
performs a card trick for passersby at the Johnson &
Johnson booth during a pharmaceutical show at the Jacob
K. Javits Convention Center in New York City.

Photograph by Kathleen Benson

Throughout American history, black magicians have achieved great skill in both the magician's tricks of the trade and in the psychology of magic. Slavery and later racial segregation and discrimination, however, have prevented most from making their living at it. Those who have succeeded are unique. Although some gained sufficient renown to have left their mark on history, many exist in historical records only as names on playbills or in newspaper advertisements. It is one of the peculiarities of U.S. history that both the first recorded American magician, Richard Potter, and one of the most celebrated magicians of the 1990s, David Blaine, are of African descent.

Richard Potter: The First American-born Magician

In the early years of European settlement in North America, there were not many public entertainments. Individuals and groups of people might get together to sing or dance, but traveling troupes that made their living by entertaining other people were rare. Towns were spread out, and there were few places with enough people to pay for amusements. In some areas, almost any form of recreation was considered a frivolous waste of time and money. In other places, it was regarded as immoral.

As the colonies grew, several early forms of entertainment became popular. By the late eighteenth century, a number of circuses were traveling about. They offered displays of horsemanship and menageries of exotic animals. They also included performances by magicians. Scholars of early American public entertainment suggest that there were at least two dozen magicians traveling around America at the time. These early magicians advertised their performances in different ways, depending on their audience. In places where pure entertainment was considered immoral, they billed their acts as educational. Where religion and morality had a looser hold on people, they promised exciting feats of trickery. The magicians who traveled around the North American colonies were from the British Isles, and the first black American magician on record was trained by a Scotsman.

Richard Potter, America's "First Negro Magician," may also have been the first American-born magician of any race. To date, no records of any earlier white American-born magicians have been discovered. Potter was born in Hopkinton, Massachusetts, in 1783, the same year the American Revolution ended.

Potter was born on the country estate of Sir Charles Henry Frankland, more commonly known as Sir Harry. Sir Harry was a wealthy Englishman who had come to the colonies as the Collector of the Port of Boston. Potter was one of five children born to Sir Harry's slave Dinah, who had been born in Africa, kidnapped as a child by Dutch slave traders, and purchased by Sir Harry at a slave auction in Boston. Dinah was apparently treated well. The American poet Oliver Wendell Holmes, who knew Sir Harry, wrote of her: "Black Dinah, stolen when a child. And sold on Boston pier. Grown up in service, petted, spoiled." Some of Dinah's children were probably fathered by Sir Harry. All were of mixed race. By the time Richard was born, however, Sir Harry had returned to England. He had remained loyal to the British cause during the Revolutionary War and returned to his homeland when it was clear the American colonists would win their independence. According to church records, Richard's father was a local white man named George Simpson. How Richard acquired Potter for a last name is not known.

Young Richard attended the village school in Hopkinton. At age ten, old enough to learn a trade, he signed on as a cabin boy with a Captain Skinner, a friend of the Frankland family. He worked only one Atlantic crossing. Arriving at the British port of Liverpool, Richard accepted his pay from Captain Skinner but told the captain that a life at sea was not for him.

Not long afterward, Richard happened on an English fair. He had never seen such an event and was fascinated by the sights and sounds. He was particularly taken with the act of a Scottish ventriloquist and magician named John Rannie. After the act was over, he hung around, hoping to talk with the Scotsman. Rannie welcomed the interest of the young mulatto boy. Coincidentally, Rannie needed a new assistant. His younger brother, James Rannie, had been working with him but had decided to strike out on his own. Richard Potter was eager to take over James's duties.

One of Rannie's most popular tricks was to cut off a chicken's head and then appear to put it back on. Among Potter's jobs as Rannie's assistant was hiding a live chicken with markings similar to the one that had been decapitated and helping Rannie switch chickens. This trick never failed to awe the crowd.

Potter traveled with Rannie around the European continent until 1800. In that year, Rannie decided to try his fortune in America, and Potter returned to his native land. Rannie billed himself as the "European Ventriloquist," and he and Potter joined up with a traveling circus. Potter also traveled to the British West Indies with Rannie.

At the time, ventriloquism was as much a mystery as magic

was to most people, and Rannie was immediately successful. His success was also due to his aggressive self-promotion. He would take out ads in the local newspapers promising to reveal the secret to one of his magic tricks at the end of his act. Since he considered himself primarily a ventriloquist, he did not mind revealing the tricks of what he considered his minor trade.

In 1801, John Rannie's brother James arrived in North America, promoting himself as the "King of Britain's Conjurers." Rather than regarding his brother as a competitor, John Rannie welcomed James as a fellow entertainer. He did, however, begin to use the stage name Rannie the Elder, to distinguish his act from that of his younger brother. At one point, Rannie the Elder and Richard Potter finished an engagement in New York City that James had begun, while James went on a tour of the South. John Rannie and Potter then went on their own tour of the South, playing Charleston, South Carolina, and Savannah, Georgia, among other cities. Because Potter was regarded as Rannie's servant by the southern whites for whom they performed, and because he behaved with modesty, he had no trouble in these areas where free blacks were looked on with suspicion.

The two met James Rannie in Philadelphia later in the year. There, Richard Potter came into contact for the first time with a large educated and prosperous black population. He also encountered racism. Realizing that blacks were as interested in magic as were whites, he persuaded Rannie to offer a special performance for the city's blacks. Rannie placed a "Notice to Coloured People" in local newspapers advertising special Tuesday night performances. The owner of the hall where they were performing objected, however, and the special performances for blacks never took place.

Not long afterward, James Rannie returned to England, leaving his elder brother, John, as the major force in American magic for almost a decade.

By 1806, John Rannie had introduced English drama into his act. He and Potter played the major roles, and Rannie hired local amateurs to play the minor parts. Their productions were titled *New Ways to Pay Old Debts*, *The Unfortunate Gentleman*, and *The Battle of the Nile*. Rannie and Potter presented the first known professional theatrical performance in English west of the Allegheny Mountains. The programs included ventriloquism by Rannie.

In 1807, Rannie and Potter returned to the Northeast and secured a booking in Boston. According to legend, they heard about a group of local Penobscot Indian fur traders who often danced to entertain the citizens in nearby Roxbury. Rannie and Potter went to see them perform and were particularly struck by one of the Penobscot women. Twenty-year-old Sally Harris was beautiful and a graceful dancer, and she sang like a bird. Rannie needed someone to play the part of Megin in their play *The Provoked Husband,* and offered the part to Sally. Potter worked with Sally to learn her lines. She did so well that she was offered a permanent position in the show. Richard Potter and Sally Harris fell in love and were married in Boston on March 25, 1808. The following year, their first son was born.

Between tours, Potter did odd jobs for the Reverend Daniel Oliver, a resident of Boston, in exchange for room and board. Potter first tried out the magic tricks he had learned performing for the children of the household in front of the Olivers' kitchen fireplace. Later on, he gathered the courage to perform a solo show in Andover, New Hampshire, at Ben Thompson's

Richard Potter used this woodcut in his advertisements.
The woodcut is amateurishly done, and it is unlikely that
its creator could have made a portrait of Potter even if he
had tried. Since birds are featured in the picture,
Potter possibly did tricks with trained fowl.

From The Illustrated History of Magic *by Milbourne Christopher and*
Maureen Christopher, courtesy of Maureen Christopher

tavern. However, he made no further attempt to strike out on
his own and remained with Rannie's act.

Rannie understood, however, that one day Potter would
have his own act. He had learned well and had the showmanship necessary to succeed. On March 7, 1810, on the stage of
the City Assembly Room in New York City, Rannie made a surprise announcement. He told his audience that he had made
enough money to return to his homeland and live comfortably.

He would soon go back to Scotland. He also announced that it was time for Richard Potter to have his own career.

Rannie's last engagement was at the Exchange Coffee House in Boston between early December 1810 and mid-January 1811. He then returned to Europe, as planned. He left Potter with a store of knowledge of ventriloquism and magic tricks. These included burning a $100-dollar bill in a candle flame and then causing it to become whole again. One hundred dollars was a tremendous amount of money in 1811, so this trick was especially popular. In another trick, he appeared to cut off the finger of a member of the audience, then reunited it with its owner. He also cut hats and handkerchiefs into pieces and then made them whole again, filled an empty bottle with water and turned it into wine, and tossed a cat into the air and made it disappear.

On November 2, 1811, Richard Potter made his debut as an independent performer at the Exchange Coffee House. With his wife, Sally, as his assistant, he performed in and around Boston, featuring ventriloquism and "one hundred curious experiments with money, eggs, cards and the like." Although most of his performances took place at the Columbian Museum, he also performed at the Exchange Coffee House and at Concert Hall and Julien Hall in that city.

Later, Richard and Sally Potter began performing in New York. According to legend, they also performed in the South, although it is hard to imagine the couple being welcomed in a part of the country where free blacks were not wanted and sometimes even legally banned.

The story goes that in Mobile, Alabama, the Potters at first were allowed to stay at the same inn where they were performing. After patrons of the inn objected, the owner of the inn refused to let them remain. The Potters were forced to sleep in the barn. Fearing for their safety, the couple left town in the middle of the night and struck off in the opposite direction from where they had announced their next show would be.

By 1814, the Potters had saved enough money to buy land and build a home for themselves and their three children—two sons and a daughter. Richard Potter chose to settle in Andover, New Hampshire, where he had first performed publicly. He bought two hundred acres of deeply forested, nearly wild land and hired a twenty-mule pack team to bring in the first farming equipment and supplies. Over time, he built a large shingled house, which came to be called the Potter Place. The second floor was one large room just for entertaining. The kitchen and bedrooms were in another building at the back of the main house. It was said that the New Hampshire legislature copied the Potter home when designing the new statehouse in Concord, which was completed in 1819.

There was much talk among the townsfolk about Potter, whom all regarded as a "furrener." Some said he was a Hindu from the East; others that he was from the West Indies. While he was too different to be entirely accepted, he and his family were never threatened. The Potters often had large dinner parties. It is said that at one of them four church elders objected to the serving of liquor. Potter cried, "If you are not tolerant of spirits, then spirits will not be tolerant of you!" whereupon he broke open a bottle to reveal a baby chick, which then looked at the elders and said "Boo!" The frightened elders ran from the house, to the delight of the other guests.

Actually, Potter was a faithful churchgoer and was one of the earliest members of the new and radical Universalist denomination of the Protestant faith. Potter was also a member of the first African Masonic Lodge, the Prince Hall Lodge in Boston, established in 1778 by Prince Hall, the black patriot of the American Revolution.

Potter's Place was a working farm, and Potter proudly listed his occupation as "Yeoman" on legal papers. He raised crops and bred horses, cattle, and pigs. He and Sally kept a large garden and were proud of the vegetables and flowers it produced. When they had time to spend at the farm, they were at their happiest, but often they had to work and could not enjoy it. Sally continued to act as her husband's assistant in his magic show, and the two were frequently on the road, leaving the farm work to hired hands.

Few people go through life without experiencing tragedy. The Potters' greatest sorrow was the loss of their seven-year-old son, Henry, who was crushed under a wagon loaded with corn in October 1816. Sally Potter never fully recovered from her grief, but she continued to work with her husband, both on the stage and on the farm.

For years, Richard Potter was the chief, and often the only, magical attraction in Boston. He advertised his performance as *An Evening's Brush to Sweep Dull Care Away* and charged twenty-five cents admission. Although he emphasized ventriloquism and was famous for his ability to "throw his voice" into pigs, horses, and people, he was also well known for his sleight-of-hand.

Richard Potter remained popular even in times when there was widespread suspicion of blacks. Throughout the period of slavery in the United States, occasional slave revolts would cause whites to suspect that magic was behind slave resistance,

The Enchanted Egg Trick

One of Richard Potter's most popular tricks was the "Enchanted Egg Trick." He placed an egg on top of a hat and made it jump to the top of another hat. He then made it jump inside one hat after the other. After that, the egg appeared on his shoulder. It rolled up and down his arms and body. Then, it suddenly disappeared.

and that put all blacks, enslaved and free, in danger. Sometimes these fears proved well grounded. In April 1712, an insurrection broke out in New York City. Twenty-seven armed slaves set fire to an outhouse and, when whites came to extinguish the fire, shot at them. Nine whites were killed before the militia was able to put down the revolt. The black men were quickly captured, tried, convicted, and executed in various ways. The plot, it was charged, had been brewed by West Africans, who "with the aid of a conjurer, believed that they had made themselves invulnerable."

In 1817, the ship *Canton* was set afire by a black man as it lay at anchor in Boston Harbor. Boston's white citizens suspected a plot. According to legend, Sally Potter, who apparently was not with him on this occasion, feared for her husband's safety in the city. She warned him that he might be run out of town, and suggested he cancel his next engagement.

Potter reportedly replied, "I am not just a colored man. I am Richard Potter, the celebrated ventriloquist." Potter was right. He had no trouble in Boston.

On August 8, 1818, Potter advertised his performance at Boston's Columbian Museum as follows:

Mr. Potter will perform the part of the anti-combustible Man Salamander [a mythical combination of human and reptile] and will pass a red hot bar of iron over his tongue, draw it through his hands repeatedly, and afterwards bend it into various shapes with his naked feet, as a smith would on an anvil. He will also immerse his hands and feet in molten lead, and pass his naked feet and arms over a large body of fire. He will also perform a variety of pleasing magical deceptions; which, to give a minute detail of, would fill a volume. The performer, not being willing to anticipate the pleasure the audience may receive from his performance, flatters himself that he is so well known in different parts of this country, as not to require the aid of a pompous advertisement. In addition to his magical and ventriloquial talents, he will introduce a number of songs and recitations.

These are some of the tricks that Potter included in his act: frying eggs in a beaver hat; thrusting a sword down his throat and drawing out yards of multicolored ribbons, then spitting out sparks and flames; appearing to swallow molten lead, using a special mixture of lead, bismuth, and block tin. He would pour the mixture into his mouth and then spit out pieces of hardened lead. Asking a member of the audience to touch the lead, he would smile when the spectator attested that it was indeed too

MULTUM IN PARVO.

AN EVENINGS BRUSH TO SWEEP AWAY CARE, OR A MEDLEY TO PLEASE

MR. POTTER,

THE VENTRILOQUIST,

Respectfully informs the Ladies and Gentlemen of
and vicinity, that his exhibition will take place at

On   Evening,

And hopes by his exertions to please, to receive the patronage of a liberal & enlightened public.

PART 1st.—Mr. POTTER will commence with his

PHILOSOPHICAL PAPER,

The Mysterious Dollars and Deceptive Ball.

THE ENCHANTED CARDS,

AND THE

MAGNETIC EGG

THAT DANCES A HORNPIPE.

After which will be presented

The Coffer of Mahomet,

OR A LADY'S GLOVE TURNED TO A LIVE BIRD.

GLASS CASKET AND MYSTERIOUS DESK,

PEXIS METALLICA,

WITH SEVERAL OTHER RECREATIONS NOT MENTIONED IN THIS BILL.

ALSO THE

TUMOROUS BALLS,

TO CONCLUDE WITH HIS

WONDERFUL FACTORY,

Which has astonished many Philosophers.

PART 2d.—Mr. POTTER will deliver his

DISSERTATION ON NOSES,

And personate the different characters of the wearers. This satirically lashes the vices and
follies of mankind, and forms a source of rational amusement.

Mr. P. will sing a number of

COMIC SONGS,

ADAPTED TO EACH CHARACTER.

PART 3d.—Mr. P. will display his wonderful, but laborious powers of

VENTRILOQUISM.

The Performance to conclude with

Tickets of admission   cts. Doors open at   and Performance to commence at   o'clock. Tickets may be had at
he har

A circular that Richard Potter used for advertising
performances in private homes. The name of his host could
be filled in at the top.

From The Illustrated History of Magic *by Milbourne Christopher and
Maureen Christopher, courtesy of Maureen Christopher*

hot to touch. Potter also put peeping chickens in women's pockets and rabbits and bumblebees in men's hats. Some said he was the best American ventriloquist and magician of his time.

It is not known how long Richard Potter continued to perform or when he retired. Perhaps he had the opportunity to enjoy his farm and his family for a few years before he died. The words inscribed on his tombstone suggest that his fame as a ventriloquist had not faded when he died. They read, "In Memory of Richard Potter, the Celebrated Ventriloquist, who died Sept. 20, 1835, aged 52 years." Sally Potter survived her husband by a little over a year. She died on October 24, 1836, at the age of forty-nine and was buried next to him.

The Potters' daughter, Jeanette, had died in 1831. The remaining child, Richard, Jr., inherited the estate. He lived there for several years before he sold it and moved on. Continuing in his father's footsteps, he performed magic, ventriloquism, song, and dance as Little Potter in New Hampshire and New York. A Henry Hatton, writing in the May 1916 issue of the magic magazine MUM, recalled that Richard Potter, Jr., was the first magician he ever saw performing at the old Olympic Theater in New York: "Little Potter, he was called. He was a young colored man, slim and graceful, and he danced and sung. One verse of his song ran: 'They call me a mulatto, And my name is Little Potter, And for cutting up the capers, I'm the dandy O.'"

There is no record of Richard, Jr., after 1840, when he last paid taxes in Troy, New York. According to some sources, he went West after that, and was never heard from again.

The name Richard Potter fell into obscurity. Then, in 1906, after seventy-one years, a G. Dana Taylor of Andover, New Hampshire, responded to an ad in Conjurer's Magazine, published by Harry Houdini. The ad requested information on "old time magicians," and Taylor, a magician who used the stage name Danar, wrote about Potter. Some of what he wrote was legend, not fact, such as that Potter was "part Hindoo." What intrigued Houdini, and other magicians, was Taylor's report of Potter's variation on the famous "Hindu Rope Trick." If true, it was the first record of an American version of the trick. The letter, published in *Conjurer's Magazine* of December 15, 1906, stated: "Before a score of people and in the open air, free from trees, houses or mechanisms, he threw up a ball of yarn and he and his wife climbed up on it and vanished in the air. A person coming up the road asked what the people were gazing at, and being told, said he met them going down the road."

In 1965, the Manchester, New Hampshire, chapter of the International Brotherhood of Magicians officially named their group, called a "ring," the Black Richard Ring in honor of America's first popular magician. Not long afterward, Old Sturbridge Village, a recreated 1830s village in Massachusetts, began to feature a magic show based on nineteenth-century magical entertainments. Robert Olson, a white engineer and maker of reproduction early American furniture from Putnam, Connecticut, researched and presented the shows. Among his most frequent historical alter-egos was Richard Potter. In 1969, he presented the act at the International Brotherhood of Magicians convention.

The 1978 *Conjuror's Journal: Excerpts from the Journal of Joshua Medley*, by Frances L. Shine, was also inspired by Potter's life.

Considering the barriers that blacks have faced throughout American history, the fact that a black man was probably the first American-born magician is quite amazing. Richard Potter was unique. And except for his son, no one lived to carry on his legacy. Not for half a century would another black American achieve fame as a magician.

Chapter 2

Henry "Box" Brown: An Escaped Slave Turned Magician

In 1848, thirteen years after Richard Potter's death, a slave named Henry Brown managed to escape to the North by being shipped in a wooden box. He became famous as Henry "Box" Brown. Brown had been an amateur magician before his escape, and many years after his daring feat, he gained fame as a professional magician.

Born in 1816 in Louisa County, Virginia, Henry Brown grew up hearing stories of the cruelties of slavery. Although he was fortunate to have a kind master, he learned early from his mother that slaves had no rights. Slave mothers often had their children taken from them and sold, and she tried to prepare Henry for that possibility.

Henry also learned at an early age legends of tricksters who managed to outwit their masters through cleverness. One of the most popular of these mythic tricksters was High John the Conqueror, whom the slaves regarded as a "hope bringer." He was a huge black man who had a large black crow as a pet and who would visit plantations and select a slave to accompany him. He would take the slave on a tour of Heaven and Hell. In some cases, the slave would then be returned to the plantation without ever having been missed; at other times, he would remain in Heaven.

Not all the clever tricksters were myths. Nearly every plantation had stories about real enslaved people who managed to play practical jokes on their fellow slaves and to get out of work by fooling—or simply charming—their masters. On the plantation where Henry Brown grew up, there was a slave named Tricky Sam, who claimed to have been a free black who was kidnapped and sold into slavery. Tricky Sam had a large repertoire of sleight-of-hand illusions, which he used to entertain his fellow slaves. Occasionally, the master would call on him to perform for the local children. Henry Brown was fascinated by Tricky Sam's ability to make bits of food disappear, and flattered by his interest, Tricky Sam taught Henry some of his tricks.

Henry Brown worked in his master's house as a servant and thus was spared the harder work of the field hands. He was treated well and even given shoes and a hat, which was uncommon. He thought himself lucky to belong to this particular master. His master was old, however. When Henry was thirteen, his master decided to prepare for his eventual death and divided his estate among his four sons. Brown became the property of a son named William who lived in Richmond, the capital of Virginia, located forty miles to the south. Soon afterward, Brown was forced to say goodbye to his mother and his siblings and to leave the only home he had ever known. He would never see it, or his family, again.

On his arrival in Richmond, Brown went before his new master, who promised to treat him well and presented him with a new set of clothes. He then went to work in his master's tobacco factory, a large business that employed 120 slaves, as well as thirty paid laborers and supervisors.

The work was hard and the days were long. The overseer, whom the slaves and paid laborers all called Mister Allen, seemed to enjoy punishing the slave laborers under his charge. He was also stealing from his employer by diverting shipments of supplies bound for the warehouse for his own use. Unfortunately, Allen had the trust of the master. Brown realized that it would do no good for him to inform the master of his overseer's activities. He fared quite well by staying out of trouble and obeying orders. He got some enjoyment from entertaining his fellow workers with the sleight-of-hand tricks he had learned back on the plantation from Tricky Sam. One trick was to place a small item, such as a nail used to seal crates of tobacco, in his hand, say an African phrase, and then open his hand to reveal an acorn.

In 1831, Allen began to deny the workers even the few privileges they had enjoyed. No more than five slaves could congregate together at one time. Black preachers were no longer permitted to visit the slaves. Only later did Brown learn that these new rules were a result of a general crackdown on slave activities following an 1831 insurrection in South Carolina led by a slave preacher named Nat Turner. Needless to say, Henry stopped doing any sleight-of-hand tricks at the warehouse. He was afraid that he would be accused of practicing witchcraft.

The following year, Brown met and fell in love with a slave

woman named Nancy, who belonged to a Mister Lee, a clerk in
a local bank. When he approached Mister Lee about marrying
Nancy, Lee informed him that he never intended to sell Nancy.
He added, however, that if Mister William would promise not
to sell Brown, the two could be married. Mister William agreed.
Since slaves were property, they could not marry legally. However, they had developed a custom, with its roots in Africa, of
jumping over a broom together to seal their vows. Henry and
Nancy jumped the broom and were thus considered married.
They remained in the separate households of their two employ-
ers but visited as often as they could.

Brown and his wife had been married about a year when
Mister Lee broke his promise and sold her. Fortunately, Nancy's
new owner, Samuel Cartrell, lived in Richmond and allowed
Brown "husbanding rights" to Nancy. The couple had three
children, and were as happy as was possible under slavery.

Late one afternoon in 1848, Brown heard the news he had
always feared. Samuel Cartrell had secretly sold Nancy and her
children to a Methodist minister from North Carolina. Brown's
family had been placed in the town prison until arrangements
could be made for them to travel to the home of their new master. Desperate, Brown went to his master and pleaded with him
for help in getting his wife and children back. The only thing
his master did was to give Brown the following morning off so
he could say goodbye to his family.

The next morning, Brown watched as five wagons were
loaded with slaves bound for North Carolina. Tearfully, he
hugged and kissed his children, who were in one of the wagons,
and then went to another wagon, where Nancy was chained
down to prevent her escape. Crying, they embraced as best they

could, and then Brown walked beside the wagon for about a mile, holding his wife's hand, until the slave drivers accompanying the caravan told him to leave.

His heart heavy with sorrow, Brown returned to the factory, praying to God for answers. As he later told the story, he was startled when a voice seemed to come to him and say, "Go get a box, and put yourself in it." Henry waited for more, but that was all. He pondered the meaning of the message and finally concluded that he was to ship himself to freedom in a wooden crate.

Like the other slaves who worked in the tobacco factory, Henry had little free time. His life was regulated from sunup to sundown, and even after. Needing time to find a box large enough to fit in, he decided to stage an "accident." He poured acid on his finger. In truth he created a real accident, as he poured too much and saw his flesh eaten away to the bone. Nevertheless, he accomplished his purpose. Allen, the overseer, sent him back to the slave quarters until he was better, but instead Brown went right to Samuel Smith's carpentry shop.

Brown knew that Smith did not believe in slavery. He explained his plan to the carpenter, and Smith agreed to construct a wooden crate three feet long, two feet wide, and two-and-a-half feet tall. He promised to have it ready in two days. He also promised to find out the best way to ship Brown to freedom.

Two days later, Brown returned to Smith's carpentry shop. The box was ready. On the outside, it looked like an ordinary shipping crate. Inside it was lined with thick woolen cloth and had three small air holes. Smith had arranged to send the box to a barber in Philadelphia who was a member of the Philadelphia Anti-Slavery Society.

Taking only an animal bladder filled with water and a few dry biscuits, Brown climbed into the box. Smith then nailed it shut and secured it with five hickory hoops. He addressed the crate to "Wm. H. Johnson, Arch Street, Philadelphia" and on the top marked it "This Side Up. Handle with Care." He also placed his return address on the crate. He was afraid of what might happen to Brown if the box did not reach its destination. By putting his own address on the crate, he risked arrest and prosecution for aiding a fugitive slave if the plot was discovered.

Smith and James C. A. Smith, a free black man who worked for him, drove the crate in a wagon to the Adams Express office. From there, it was taken to the railroad depot, where it was loaded onto a train. It was transferred from the train to a steamboat, along with bags of mail. The workers who moved the crate from one place to another paid no attention to the warning This Side Up on the crate. More than once, Brown found himself traveling upside down, the blood rushing to his head, causing his eyes to swell and his veins to protrude. At such times, he would pray to God to stay alive.

By the time Henry Brown's box reached Philadelphia, it was three o'clock in the morning. The box had traveled a distance of 350 miles, and the trip had taken twenty-six hours. For six hours more, Brown's box sat in the Philadelphia train depot. Fortunately, it was upright, and so was Brown inside it. He had long since finished the food and water he had brought with him, and having nowhere to relieve himself, he was soaking wet and very unpleasant smelling.

The following morning, an Adams Express driver delivered the box to William H. Johnson. The barber was expecting the crate, and other members of the Philadelphia Anti-Slavery So-

Henry Brown emerging from the box in which he
was shipped from slavery in Richmond, Virginia,
to freedom in Philadelphia.

ciety were waiting with him. They had no way of knowing if
Brown had survived the trip. Before opening the crate, they
rapped on it and asked, "Is all right within?"

From the box came the response, "All right."

The men cut the hickory hoops that held the box closed
and removed the lid. Out stepped Henry Brown. "How do you
do, gentlemen," he said, then passed out.

When he revived, Brown told the men that he had promised
God that if he survived the journey, he would sing the "Hymn of
Thanksgiving." He then launched into "I waited patiently for
the Lord, and He heard my prayer." He was exhausted, bruised,
and soaked with urine, but he had made it to freedom.

Henry Brown hoped that one day he could somehow find
and free his wife and children. He could not risk returning to

the South, however. For the time being, the best he could do was work for the antislavery cause so that others could be free as well. As Henry "Box" Brown, he became a popular speaker at antislavery meetings. With the help of Charles Stearns, an abolitionist editor, he put his story down on paper. In September 1849, Stearns published *Narrative of Henry Box Brown, Who Escaped from Slavery Enclosed in a Box 3 Feet Long and 2 Feet Wide*. Brown saved as much as he could of the fees he earned from his lectures and the proceeds from the sale of his book. He was determined to purchase his wife and children from slavery.

Meanwhile, back in Richmond, Samuel Smith and his employee, James Smith, boxed up two other slaves and delivered them to the Adams Express depot. Unfortunately, a slave hunter searching for runaway slaves happened to check the depot and discovered the plot. Samuel Smith was arrested. Tried and convicted of aiding fugitive slaves, he was imprisoned until 1856. James C. A. Smith was also arrested, but he was later released. Even though he had helped his employer, he was judged to have been coerced into doing so and thus not responsible for the crime. Nevertheless, Smith feared for his life and fled Richmond in late 1849 to join Henry Brown, who was living in New Bedford, Massachusetts.

Not long afterward, Brown and Smith began traveling with a huge painting entitled *Mirror of Slavery*. Called a panorama, the painting depicted a variety of scenes of slave life and slave escapes, including one of Brown's escape in a box. It served as the backdrop for an antislavery performance. A black man from Boston named Benjamin F. Roberts wrote a narration and introduced the program. Brown and Smith told of their experiences. The program was presented in many New England cities.

In 1850, the same year as the traveling panorama show began, Congress passed a fugitive slave act. Much stronger than the first such act passed in 1793, it permitted federal officers to seize fugitives anywhere in the United States, making it easier to capture and return escaped slaves to their owners. On August 30, Henry Brown was with the *Mirror of Slavery* exhibit in Providence, Rhode Island, when none other than Mister Allen, the overseer of the Richmond tobacco factory, arrived in the company of a professional slave hunter.

The two men pushed through the crowd and confronted Henry. The slave hunter pointed a gun at his chest, and the helpless Brown doubted he could survive if he ran. Fortunately, James Smith was outside the exhibit and heard the confrontation. Thinking quickly, he started calling out to the crowd, "For the next five minutes, people are welcome to enter the panorama free of charge! Free admission now!" A swarm of people rushed in, jostling the slave hunters, giving Henry an opportunity to duck beneath the canvas. He leaped astride a nearby horse and galloped away. He rode to the home of the Providence abolitionist who had sponsored the panorama in that city. James Smith joined him there.

That frightening brush with recapture convinced Henry Brown that he was no longer safe in the United States. Brown and Smith had heard that there was a strong abolitionist movement in England, where slavery had been outlawed in 1833. They decided to take the panorama across the Atlantic. The man who had originally commissioned the panorama allowed them to take it abroad, but he would not pay for the trip. Brown was forced to use the money he had been saving to buy freedom for his wife and children to pay for his passage to the English port city of Liverpool. From there, they took the panorama on a tour of the British Isles. To publicize the tour, Brown would arrange to have himself shipped in a box from one stop on the tour to another. James Smith would open the box, and Henry would step out, to the delight of the assembled crowd.

After a while, Smith demanded a full partnership in the *Mirror of Slavery* enterprise. When Brown refused, Smith left. He set out on his own tour, billing himself as "Boxer Smith, the man who boxed Henry Brown."

In 1861, the American Civil War began. While North and South fought over the questions of slavery, states rights, and economic issues, Henry Brown remained in England. Even after the North was victorious in the war, and slavery was abolished by the Thirteenth Amendment to the U.S. Constitution, Brown stayed abroad. With the *Mirror of Slavery* panorama, he joined other touring shows.

Magicians were often part of these touring shows. Brown was interested in their acts because of his early fascination with magic tricks, but he was especially interested in their escape tricks. After a time, Brown added a new twist to his story of es-caping slavery in a wooden crate. He began to feature an act in which he was closed up in a large canvas sack. A chain was wrapped around it, secured by a heavy padlock. Brown delight-ed crowds wherever he went by managing to free himself in less than five minutes.

As time went on, Brown featured more and more magic in

The Spirit Cabinet

One of Brown's most popular escape tricks was called "The Spirit Cabinet." He would ask a member of the audience to tie his hands and feet. His assistant then placed him behind a curtain with a tray holding a bugle, a dinner bell, and a tambourine. From behind the curtain soon came the sounds of the bell and instruments. Yet after Brown called out for the curtain to be pulled open, he would be revealed still bound by the ropes. Although he would then explain that it had all been a trick, he would not reveal how he had done it.

his program. He created his own show, entitled *Mesmeric Entertainments*, and toured with it successfully for a quarter century.

At last, around 1875, Henry Brown returned to the United States. Billing himself as Professor H. Box Brown, he toured the Northeast with a program entitled *The African Prince's Drawing Room Entertainment*. He had a wife, listed in playbills only as Madame Brown, whose specialty was "The Mysterious Second Sight Performance," and a daughter, listed as Miss Annie Brown, whose act was advertised as "Wonderful Sack Feat by Miss Annie Brown, such as was never performed before by any child." Nothing else is known about this second family. There is also no record of what became of his first wife, Nancy, and their children.

Brown advertised his program as "First class European entertainment" and included a number of standard tricks of the magic trade. He borrowed a handkerchief from a member of his audience, set it on fire, and then restored it. He placed a seed in a container, covered it with a cup, and produced a bouquet of flowers. He shuffled a pack of cards, asked three members of the audience to each select one card, show the rest of the spectators, and then replace it. Brown then tossed the pack of cards in the air, stabbing at the flutter of cards with a sword. When the rest of the cards had fallen to the floor, the three cards selected by the audience volunteers were impaled on the sword's blade.

Brown borrowed a pocket watch from an audience volunteer. He then placed the watch in a box and locked the box, putting the key on the owner's watch fob. Brown made magical gestures over the box, then asked the volunteer to open it. The audience, seeing that the box was empty, would gasp. Brown would then ask the volunteer to remove his hat. Reaching inside the hat, Brown would produce the watch.

Brown's last known performance was in Lynn, Massachusetts, in 1878, when he was sixty-two years old. He advertised his act as including:

Destroying and restoring a Handkerchief, astounding feat with the Sword and Cards, the wonderful Flying Card and Box Feat, Burning Cards and Restoring them again, the wonderful experiment of passing a Watch through a number of Boxes, the extraordinary feat of Flying Money, the Inexhaustible Pan, the instantaneous Growth of Flowers, the Enchanted Glass, etc., etc.

A number of twentieth-century sources have identified this portrait as that of an older Henry "Box" Brown. However, it is more likely a sketch of Anthony Burns, the most celebrated victim of the Fugitive Slave Act of 1850. Burns was an escaped slave who was captured in Boston and returned to slavery in Virginia—a story similar to Brown's frightening brush with recapture. (Burns's freedom was later purchased by northern abolitionist friends.) This same image, with slightly more of the torso showing, is used on the cover of an 1864 pamphlet about the Anthony Burns trial.

Courtesy of Jim Magus

Mr. Brown, having only just returned to this country from England, will give a first-class European Entertainment.

It is not known what became of Henry Brown after that last known performance. The man who held the rare distinction of being famous twice—once for his daring escape from slavery and a second time as a successful magician—died in obscurity.

Chapter
3

Minstrel Magicians

By the time Henry Brown returned to the United States from Europe, there were far more opportunities for black entertainers in the land of his birth. The northern victory in the Civil War brought the end of slavery as well as amendments to the U.S. Constitution that were intended to guarantee equal rights to blacks. Although blacks were treated as second-class citizens—and in some areas as virtual slaves—they at least could travel around without fear of being captured and enslaved, or re-enslaved. Blacks were able to participate in popular entertainments and tour with performing shows.

One of those forms of entertainment was minstrelsy. This first truly American contribution to the history of entertainment was patterned after slave performances on southern plantations. Every plantation of any size had its talented slave dancers, singers, and comedians, who performed for visitors and

By the time blacks were allowed into minstrelsy, the minstrel formula was so firmly established that they often had to wear blackface makeup just as white minstrels did. This was true even in all-black musicals, like the 1903 *In Dahomey*. This photograph of a scene from the musical includes the well-known team of Bert Williams (left) and George Walker (wearing blackface makeup), with George's wife, Adah. Women were rare in minstrelsy, because their presence was believed not to fit with the buffoonery expected of the form.

at festivals. By the early 1800s, some white performers had begun to imitate these slave entertainments, even blackening their faces with burnt cork, or "blackface" makeup. Real minstrelsy that focused on the Negro as a source of theatrical material did not begin until the late 1820s. At that time, a little-known white performer named Thomas Rice happened to see an old slave named Daddy Jim Crow do a funny song and dance. Rice was delighted with the old man's performance and immediately decided to take on not just the comical song and dance but also the old man's name. Daddy Jim Crow Rice was an immediate hit, and his act spawned dozens of imitations. The name "Jim Crow" was later applied to laws and customs that segregated, or separated, blacks from whites. For example, segregated streetcars were called "Jim Crow" cars.

By the middle 1850s, whole shows were built on imitations of black performances and minstrelsy was born. A minstrel show consisted of three acts. The first was a comedy routine. The second, called the "olio," offered a variety of performances, from songs and dances, to banjo playing, to performing animals, to magic and ventriloquism. The third act, called the "after-piece" or "after-part," also featured several acts, including take-offs on popular plays, operas, and important persons.

From start to finish, the minstrel show depended on the Negro, or on white perceptions of the Negro. Instruments preferred by blacks were played. These included the banjo, which had been brought by slaves from West Africa. The dances and songs were imitations of black dances and songs. The dialogue was an imitation of black dialect. Blacks themselves remained banned from minstrelsy for the most part, although there were exceptions in northern cities where abolitionism was strong. Not until after the Civil War were more than a handful of black performers allowed onto the minstrel stage. By that time, the formula for the minstrel show was so firmly established that they were stuck with it. Blacks were forced to do what amounted to an imitation of an imitation of plantation slave life. They even had to perform in blackface makeup. And they had to continue the often cruel stereotypes that had been set by white minstrelsy.

One of the negative nicknames for a black person was "coon." In the late nineteenth and early twentieth centuries, "Coon songs" were very popular. The song "All Coons Look Alike to Me," with words and music by the talented black star of the musical stage, Ernest Hogan, contained this chorus:

> All coons look alike to me,
> I've got another beau, you see,
> And he's just as good to me as you, nig! ever tried to be,
> He spends his money free, I know we can't agree,
> So I don't like you no how,
> All coons look alike to me.

The black singer Sissieretta Jones had a troupe called the Black Patti Company, which in 1897 featured a show called *At Jolly Coon-ey Island*. The following year, another black troupe, John W. Isham's Octoroons, performed a farce called *A Tenderloin Coon*.

Of course, black performers hated having to use this insulting word and to perform stereotypical roles. Nevertheless, the only way they could succeed in show business was to do so. They found ways to maintain their dignity while publicly acting the fool. When a young man asked the legendary black comedian Billy Kersands how he could bring himself to put a whole cup and saucer in his mouth in front of whites, Kersands responded, "Son, if they hate me, I'm still whipping them, because I'm making them laugh."

Magic and ventriloquism had long been part of the olio portion of the minstrel show, and many black magicians now seized the opportunity to go on the stage. More often than not, they had learned their skills by serving as assistants to white magicians. The greatest white magician of the late nineteenth century was Alexander Herrmann, who billed himself as Herrmann the Great. He always had a black assistant who provided comic relief, and that assistant, no matter what his real name, was always called "Boomsky."

M. H. EVERETT

M. H. (Milton Hutchin) Everett was the last Boomsky. It is not known when he was born, but he apparently got his start in magic as a teenager in 1895. In that year, a white magician named Frederick Bancroft hired him to perform as his comedic assistant. Everett proved to be a great comedian who often stole the show. With Bancroft, he reputedly toured Europe and India as well as the United States. During the summer months, when Bancroft took a vacation, Everett, who was no slouch as a magician but had little opportunity to display his skills in Bancroft's act, performed a magic act of his own for black churches and clubs.

Bancroft died in Charleston, South Carolina, in 1897. A member of the Herrmann company then approached Everett and offered him the job of Boomsky. Everett eagerly accepted. He had toured with Herrmann for a little over a year when Alexander Herrmann died in late 1896. Luckily, Everett was not out of a job. Herrmann's wife, Adelaide, who also performed in the Herrmann the Great show, then summoned her

Milton Hutchin Everett was the last of Herrmann the
Great's Boomskys. After Herrmann's death, Everett
remained with the show, assisting Herrmann's nephew.
When the show broke up, he performed as a solo act in
minstrel shows, combining comedy with magic.

Courtesy of Jim Magus

nephew, Leon, from France to take over the starring role. M. H. Everett stayed on as Boomsky.

In December 1898, a magazine called *Mahatma* carried a photograph of Everett, a handsome, dark-skinned young man in tuxedo and white tie.

> "Everett the Magician, known professionally as Boomskie [*sic*], is a well-known and clever assistant to Herrmann. . . . Mr. Everett has all the qualifications that go to make up the quick witted assistant who at all times is able to cover up and help out in case of an accident in the workings of the professor's problems. He was an assistant to the late Bancroft, and was with him until his death. . . . Herrmann's entertainment was not complete without seeing Boomskie, who is a clever comedian in the part he plays upon the stage. His mimicry is perfect and his actions were all so natural that he became a great favorite with the Herrmann the Great Co."

Leon and his aunt Adelaide performed together only until the end of the 1898–1899 season. At the beginning of the next season, Leon brought in his wife, Marie, to replace Adelaide Herrmann on the program. Adelaide brought suit against Leon to stop his use of the Herrmann the Great title, but she was unsuccessful. She then struck out on her own and enjoyed a long career in vaudeville.

Leon did not have the talent or stage presence of his late uncle, and without Adelaide Herrmann's show-business sense to guide him, he did not do well. Although he continued with his show for several years, he was eventually reduced to per-

The Transformed Handkerchief

Everett had a keen comic sense and added much to the Herrmann the Great show. One of their most popular routines was called "The Transformed Handkerchief." Herrmann would borrow a handkerchief from a member of the audience and then toss it to Boomsky. By the time it reached Boomsky, it would be in shreds. Complaining loudly, Boomsky would take out a needle and thread and try to sew the pieces back together. Instead of the original square piece of fabric, however, he would produce a long strip. A growling Herrmann would snatch it back, load it into a blunderbuss, and shoot the gun at a lemon. He would then cut open the lemon and pull the restored handkerchief out of it. Then Boomsky would accidentally set the handkerchief on fire. The routine could go on and on, with the magician and his assistant arguing over who was to blame for the various mishaps and the audience howling with laughter.

forming in vaudeville with an abbreviated version of the big show. At some point, M. H. Everett left the Herrmann the Great show and formed an independent act, taking the stage name Boomsky the Magician. He joined Pringle's Minstrels and traveled with them throughout the Midwest. He usually opened the second portion of the program. One advertisement billed

him as "the Great Boomsky, pulpet [*sic*] of Herman the Great."
(It was probably supposed to read pupil.)

Although Everett now had the opportunity to feature his
skills as a magician and downplay his skills as a comedian, he
found that a combination of the two was the most successful.
His most famous routine was the "Human Chicken," a variation
on an egg trick he had performed while assisting Herrmann. He
would walk out on stage bent over at the waist, with his hands
tucked into his armpits and his elbows flapping in the air.
Clucking like a chicken, he would produce an egg from his
mouth. Then he would produce another egg, and then another
and another. He placed the eggs on a tray. One of the eggs
would suddenly fall and break, and Everett would look wide-
eyed at the audience, which dissolved into laughter at his pan-
tomimed humiliation. He then produced one last egg from his
mouth and held it up, as if threatening to throw it into the audience. He lobbed it out above the audience's heads, where in
mid-air it turned into a hail of confetti.

Everett left Pringle's Minstrels in 1909. He continued to
perform in other minstrel shows until 1925, when he retired
to Truro, Nova Scotia. He returned to the United States in
February 1932 to attend the funeral of Alexander Herrmann's
widow, Adelaide. Speaking tearfully at the service, Everett
said, "A golden age of vaudeville goes with her, and there are
few enough who remember it now." It is not known when
M. H. Everett died.

ALONZO MOORE

Like M. H. Everett, Alonzo Moore was also associated with Alexander Herrmann. Moore never worked as Herrmann's assistant, but the press labeled him "the Black Herrmann," favorably comparing him to that great white magician.

Little is known about Moore's life. The only sources about him are newspaper references to his performances. His career makes him worth discussing here, but his personal life is a mystery. We do not know when he was born. A 1906 newspaper article describes him as "young."

Moore began his career as Theosis, the assistant to white magician Edward Maro, who billed himself the Prince of Magic. After Maro married in April 1899, his wife, Allie May Kaiser, took over as his assistant. Moore left the act and for a time performed at the Clark Street Museum in Chicago. He then began a long period of touring with various minstrel shows, performing comedy, pantomime, and magic tricks that he had learned from Maro.

In 1903, Moore was with a troupe called the Hottest Coon in Dixie Company, which billed him as the Black Demon. The following year, he joined the Cotton Belt Jubilee Singers. With this group, Moore performed a magic act in the olio portion of the performance that one reviewer praised highly: "Without a doubt Alonzo Moore will be the leading colored magician before the public." Other companies with which Moore traveled were Pringle's Georgia Minstrels and Lowery's Greater Minstrels, an all-black troupe of forty people that played throughout the South.

Moore's comedy was almost as popular as his magic. He

Like many other black magicians in the late nineteenth
and early twentieth centuries, Alonzo Moore started out as
an assistant to a white magician. After he began to perform
on his own, one of his best-known acts was the
"Multiplying Billiard Balls," in which he would make pool
balls appear, disappear, and multiply in his fingers.

Courtesy of Mike Caveney's Magic Words

The Multiplying Billiard Balls
and Flags of the World

Two of the tricks Alonzo Moore learned from Edward Maro and successfully included his act were sleight-of-hand routines. In the "Multiplying Billiard Balls," Moore would make pool balls appear and disappear and multiply in his fingers, all the while looking comically wide-eyed as if surprised by his own abilities. Suddenly, a ball would disappear from his fingers and reappear in his mouth. "Flags of the World" had been Maro's climactic illusion, and it became Moore's as well. He would suddenly produce a ribbon holding flags of all nations that stretched across the stage. To the delight of the audience, the final flag would be the American flag.

spoke in broad Negro dialect and acted the stereotype of the northern "dandy" who dresses in gaudy clothes, misuses big words, and thinks only of having a good time. His talent was particularly appreciated by the most famous black comedian of the day, Billy Kersands.

Kersands, whose mouth was so large he could put a cup and saucer into it, had just formed his own minstrel troupe in 1904 when he approached Moore about bringing his magic act to the new show. Moore left the Cotton Belt Jubilee Singers and joined the Billy Kersands Minstrels.

The troupe performed in cities across the Midwest. In its review of the February 20, 1906, performance in Indianapolis, the *Indianapolis Freeman*, a black newspaper, declared:

> Alonzo Moore, a young magician whose racial accent gave the audience pleasure, soon convinced them that he was up to the usual standard of his race in another line. From tiny bits of paper he made ribbons, throwing them all over the audience. At other moments he produced chickens, jack rabbits and guinea pigs without notice. The sudden production of flags of all nations, including a large American, was something to wonder at and won for him great applause.

In November of that year, the troupe traveled to New Orleans, where Kersands had arranged to lease the Elysium Theatre for a week. The theater's usual policy was to allow blacks to sit only on one side of the upper balcony. During the week of Kersands' show, however, that policy was reversed, and whites were confined to that balcony. The show was heavily advertised in the black community, and thousands attended in the course of the week. Whites were so eager to see the show that they accepted the uncommon restrictions on them; at the November 10 performance, 150 whites sat in the balcony.

Since the show played sold-out houses wherever it went, Kersands was able to hire his own private train coach. Moore invested in a special backdrop for his magic act—a hand-painted scene of a wizard's cave. He also hired an assistant. In his review of the Billy Kersands Minstrels show at the Grand

Opera House in Hazelton, Pennsylvania, on March 9, 1907, Sylvester Russell of the *Indianapolis Freeman* wrote:

> Alonzo Moore, the black Herman [sic] has elaborated his act this season. The stage was set in a scene described as 'Cave of the Wizard,' taken from Demon's Gulch, Death Valley. The cabinet scenes of his act were especially mystifying, especially where ducks appeared in an empty box. Mr. Moore's Negro dialect oratory is very entertaining and he is as quick as the ticking of an alarm clock with his magic temerity. On the contrary, he was assisted by a valet who is much too slow for the good of his business.

Moore remained with the Billy Kersands Minstrels for five seasons. He was with the group when they toured in Europe and played a command performance in London for Queen Victoria. By the time the show returned to the United States, Kersands and Moore had either tired of operating their own show or had run into financial difficulties. In 1909 they closed the show and together joined Pringle's Georgia Minstrels. Three years later, Moore was with Lowery's Greater Minstrels. The following year, 1913, Moore was again with Billy Kersands as part of the Hugo Brothers Minstrels, who were on tour in Honolulu, Hawaii.

According to Jim Magus, author of *Magical Heroes: The Lives and Legends of Great African American Magicians*, Black Herman (a black magician featured in Chapter 7) said Moore died in 1914. If that is correct, then Moore had a short life and an even shorter career. Based on the evidence of the newspaper reviews, however, and on his relationship with the acclaimed Billy Kersands, he was successful in his chosen field.

Chapter 4

William Carl on
the Vaudeville Stage

By the time Alonzo Moore is said to have died in 1914, minstrelsy had gone out of fashion. In fact, its popularity had begun to wane even before Moore entered show business.

By the 1880s, many minstrel shows had become rowdy and sometimes vulgar entertainments that respectable citizens avoided. Vaudeville arose as a more tasteful popular amusement form. The forerunner of the modern variety show, vaudeville had distinctly urban roots, as opposed to the southern plantation flavor of classic minstrelsy. B. F. Keith opened the first vaudeville theater in Boston in 1882. He demanded that the acts he booked conform to very rigid standards. Every word spoken or sung, every costume and gesture, had to be in good taste. Nothing vulgar or off-color was allowed. Performers at Keith's theater offered popular music, comedy, and variety acts that drew a wide audience, including women and children.

This photograph of an unidentified black vaudeville group
shows how the form represented a step up from minstrelsy.
Vaudeville, which was the forerunner of the modern variety
show, was a more tasteful popular amusement form that
welcomed women and emphasized glamour over buffoonery.

*Courtesy of Schomburg Center for Research in Black Culture, The New York
Public Library, Astor, Lenox, and Tilden Foundations*

By 1893, B. F. Keith had opened a vaudeville house in New
York City, and soon he had a network of theaters from the East
Coast to Chicago. Martin Beck's Orpheum Circuit controlled
major vaudeville houses west and south of Chicago. Vaudeville
had supplanted minstrelsy as America's major popular entertainment form. Although some entertainers complained that
vaudeville was boring and bland, they were forced to change
with the times.

William Carl was among the black entertainers who successfully made the transition from minstrelsy to vaudeville.
Like those of so many other black entertainers who worked in

the late nineteenth and early twentieth centuries, William Carl's origins and personal life are obscure. His name, however, can be found often in lists of performers and reviews of variety shows. Like most entertainers of the time, he moved around a lot.

In the earliest record of Carl, around 1890, he is billed as the King of the Magicians with a minstrel troupe called Boston's Merry Musicians. The troupe was a "class act" whose members dressed in white tuxedos. Carl himself favored a cutaway jacket, vest, and knee breeches, with hose and black shoes with silver buckles.

Perhaps because of his early travels with a musical troupe, Carl developed a type of magic routine different from that of most minstrel magicians—a classier act that included music. For an example, he would show his audience a spoon, which he would then drop into a glass bottle. He would cork the bottle and then gesture to the spoon as if conducting an orchestra. The spoon would dance to the music played by the show's band.

Carl was with Sam T. Jack's Creole Company, billed as Black Carl, the Magician, in September 1896. A month later, he was still with Jack's company, but billed as Black Carl, the Creole Mahatma (see Chapter 6 for an explanation of this type of stage name). By July of the following year, he was performing with John W. Vogel's Darkest America Company as Black Carl, Hoodoo Magician. Among the tricks he performed were producing roses in a vase; changing coffee beans into a cup of steaming coffee; coughing up feathers, first, and then a whole baby chick. He also would place a sliver of chalk between two slates, make

The only known photograph of William Carl is of such poor quality that it is hard to make out. It shows him in formal dress, apparently doing a trick, although it is impossible to tell what illusion he is performing.

Courtesy of Jim Magus

some gestures over the slates, and then separate them to reveal messages written on the surfaces of the slates.

By late September 1897, Carl had joined a show called *A Trip to Coontown*. Written by two black entertainers, Bob Cole and Billy Johnson, the show was the first to be entirely organized, written, produced, and managed by blacks. It was also the first musical show with an overall plot that carried one group of characters from beginning to end. At first, the company, which consisted of eighteen players, performed in the worst houses in every city. By the time the show opened at the Third Avenue Theatre in New York City in 1898, however, it had become wildly popular.

Carl left the show around that time. Although it was successful, he took the opportunity to join the most popular black team of the day, Bert Williams and George Walker. By October 1898, he was a member of Williams and Walker's Senegambian Company, billed again as Black Carl, the Magician. Carl remained with Williams and Walker for some time, performing in whatever show they happened to put on for which they needed a magician. One such show was performed by Williams and Walker's Lucky Coon Company, at Chicago's Park Theatre in December 1898.

In 1899, Carl got the opportunity to travel abroad when he joined the white promoter M. B. Curtis's Afro-American Minstrel Carnival on an international tour. Curtis's troupe was large, numbering dozens of individual performers, N. Clark Smith's Piccaninny Band, and a production staff of seven. Carl was in highly talented company, including Ernest Hogan, "The Unbleached American," who was famous for his song "All Coons Look Alike to Me." In a letter to the New York City newspaper *The Clipper*, Hogan described the troupe's itinerary:

Left N.Y. City May 23, arriving in Vancouver, B.C. 29th of May. Sailed June 1 for Honolulu where we arrived June 9 and gave a matinee and night show. Left for Sura, Fiji Islands, on June 9 at 11 P.M. and arrive Sura on Sunday June 18th. Stayed there for 6 hours and arrived in Brisbane, Australia, Saturday, 25th June. Arrive in Sydney, Tuesday, 27th June, 11 A.M. Opened in Sydney, Saturday July 1 against competition of McAdoo's Georgia Minstrels. Closed Sydney, Saturday, July 29. Open at Auckland, New Zealand, Aug. 15th.

During that tour, a white American magician, Oscar Eliason, who went by the stage name Dante the Great, was killed in a shooting accident in New South Wales. His widow, Edmunda, took advantage of the publicity surrounding her late husband's death and performed in Sydney and Melbourne as Madame Dante before she returned to the United States. Eliason's brother, Frank, followed suit. He took his brother's stage name and got bookings in New Zealand and the Philippines.

William Carl also sensed the current advantage of associating himself with the late white magician while he was in Australia and began billing himself as Black Dante. In the program of M. B. Curtis's Afro-American Minstrel Carnival for the Opera House in Wellington, New Zealand, Carl was the first performer in the olio portion of the show, listed as Black Dante (The Original Dante the Great). According to the New Zealand newspaper *Evening Post*, Black Dante's art was "of the 'right color' and mystifying." In its review of the show, the newspaper reported: "'The Black Dante' held a seance, and in the performance of tricks he compared by no means unfavorably with the conjurer from Salt Lake City [meaning the late Dante the Great, Oscar Eliason] who was recently in Wellington."

As the century turned, relationships between M. B. Curtis and his performers soured. In late January 1900, members of the troupe sued Curtis for nonpayment of salary, and a court in

Christchurch, New Zealand, judged in favor of the cast. Rather than pay the performers what he owed them, Curtis fled the country. Newspaper coverage of the incident resulted in financial assistance from home and an offer from McAdoo's Georgia Minstrels, which was also playing Australia and New Zealand at the time, to join that troupe. Several members of the Curtis show accepted the McAdoo company's offer. Ernest Hogan and William Carl decided instead to take advantage of the publicity they had received as a result of being stranded to form their own company. They reorganized the company as Hogan's Afro-American Minstrels, with Hogan as the star of the show and Carl as both a performer and the troupe's business manager. They traveled from New Zealand to Honolulu, Hawaii, a city that was just recovering from an outbreak of plague.

There, the Hogan troupe encountered another kind of plague, that of racism. So deeply ingrained were white prejudices against blacks that even high praise for black entertainers was insulting and offensive—for example, this review from the March 17, 1900, issue of the local newspaper, the *Pacific Commercial Advertiser*: "As a fitting finish to the plague and its privations come Ernest Hogan's colored minstrels to the Orpheum. All is not lost when we can get a real 'coony' coon show; Honolulu has always had a partiality for the jolly and happy-go-lucky fun of the minstrel troupe." In the same article, William Carl was singled out for special mention as "one of the best magicians of the age, the color line apart."

Four days later, in the article "Ernest Hogan's Minstrels," the *Pacific Commercial Advertiser* stated: "It certainly seems more like old times, now that the Orpheum is again in full blast. One good thing about the house is the fact that practically every cent paid for admission remains in town. Vaudeville artists are proverbially spendthrifts; who ever heard of a 'coon' keeping his money?"

The company gave what was billed as its farewell performance in Honolulu on April 9. Carl introduced some new tricks, including a version of his "Spirit Cabinet" routine, and Hogan some new songs. Two nights later, the troupe was due to sail for Vancouver on the ship *Miowera*, operated by the Canadian-Australian Royal Mail Steamship Company. When ship personnel saw that the company's members were black, they refused to allow them aboard.

As the company's business manager, William Carl went to the steamship office in an attempt to resolve the problem. When he got nowhere, he asked for help from the manager of the Orpheum Theatre, where the troupe had been performing. The manager proved to have no influence. The *Miowera* steamed out of Honolulu Harbor without the Hogan troupe, who were left on the dock with their baggage, scenery, and equipment, and minus the two thousand dollars they had paid for their tickets.

The stranded Hogan company sued the steamship line, filing twenty-nine separate suits, and paying the filing costs of twenty-seven dollars per suit because they were determined to fight for their rights. In the meantime, they continued to perform at the Orpheum. Advertisements for the show trumpeted that it had been held over by "popular demand." William Carl commented wryly, "Yes, the popular demand aboard the *Miowera*'s crew that colored folk not travel in their vessel!"

On May 1, 1900, a Honolulu court found in favor of the Hogan troupe, assessing $2,250 in damages against the steamship company. On May 26, the troupe finally set sail for Vancouver, British Columbia.

Arriving back on the North American mainland, William Carl left the Hogan troupe. He signed on with Hertig and Seamon, a white vaudeville booking agency, for a tour in which he was billed as Black Carl Dante. Aided by two assistants, Midget Price and Little Chick, he performed his magic act for one season on primarily white stages. He then rejoined Williams and Walker. He used the management skills he had learned while with the Hogan troupe on the Pacific tour to co-manage, with Charles H. Moore, Williams and Walker's show *A Lucky Coon*. He also performed his magic act as part of the show.

Bert Williams was fascinated with Carl's card tricks, and Carl obligingly taught the comedian his secrets, which Williams then used in his act. Unfortunately, Williams committed the grave crime of revealing the secrets of the tricks to the audience, causing great upset among professional magicians and embarrassing William Carl.

Ernest Hogan had in the meantime taken his troupe back to Hawaii. He'd asked Carl to accompany the show as business manager and entertainer. Carl had turned him down, unwilling to return to a place that held such painful memories. By the time the Hogan troupe got back to the United States, it had been reorganized as the Jolly Set Company. Hogan again approached Carl about joining him, and this time Carl accepted. Black Carl Dante was listed as the stager of *Belle of Darktown* when the Jolly Set Company performed that show in Waterbury, Connecticut, in July 1903. In October of the same year, the company performed *A Bogus Prince* at Proctor's 23rd Street Theatre in New York City; Carl was listed on the program as a magician.

The Inexhaustible Bottle

William Carl's signature trick was "The Inexhaustible Bottle." He would pour different-colored liquids from a bottle, then open the bottom of the bottle to remove a succession of scarves, all of them dry, in colors matching the colors of the liquids. From time to time, he changed the routine. At one point, he would climax it by breaking open the end of the bottle and producing a white rat.

For the next six years, William Carl managed and performed in a variety of shows, primarily in white vaudeville theaters. Blacks were finding it more and more difficult to appear on white stages, however. A wave of vicious antiblack sentiment swept the country in the early years of the twentieth century. It was the result of many things, but in general it was a response to a new generation of black Americans who had never experienced slavery. They were not as timid around whites as their parents and grandparents had been. They were not as likely to remain in virtual slavery on southern farms. In 1896, a newspaper in Louisiana declared, "The negroes are being overbearing and need toning down."

That year, a New Orleans mulatto named Homer Plessy sued a Louisiana railroad company for forcing him to sit in its Jim Crow car. The case of *Plessy* v. *Ferguson* went all the way to the U.S. Supreme Court, which ruled that separate public accommodations were constitutional as long as they were equal. That "separate but equal" decision by the highest court in the land opened the way for a system of legal segregation that would last for more than sixty years.

Antiblack resentment was not confined to the South. In northern cities, immigrants from Europe found themselves competing with blacks for jobs. Across the nation, there were riots against blacks and scores of lynchings—or illegal executions of blacks by white mobs.

Traditionally, the entertainment field is more accepting of differences among people than is the general public. This era of antiblack sentiment was an exception because it also infected entertainment. A white theatrical association named the White Rats mounted a campaign to bar black performers from major white vaudeville circuits, and bookings became more difficult to get. In New York City, the entertainment capital of the nation, a racial incident at the rooftop theater Jardin de Paris in 1909 resulted in blacks' being barred from theaters in New York.

William Carl and others decided to take action. That September, the Colored Vaudeville Benevolent Association was organized in New York City. In early October, Carl and a fellow performer, George Archer, opened New York's first black vaudeville theater, the Palace Hall Theatre at 51st Street and Seventh Avenue, in the heart of Manhattan's black community. Modeled on all-black theaters in other cities, such as the Pekin in Chicago, the Palace Hall presented "refined white comedies," rather than the stereotyped "coon shows" that blacks had been forced to perform for so long. Unlike the Pekin, however, the Palace Hall did not last long.

What happened to William Carl after that is not known.

When he disappeared from the pages of white newspapers, he became invisible. He was still active and trying to make a success of the Palace Hall Theatre when Harry Houdini wrote in the December 1909 issue of his *Conjurer's Magazine:* "Black Carl was once frequently heard of, but at the present date a colored magician is an actual novelty."

The "colored" magician was actually less a novelty than Houdini realized. Black magicians had responded to racism and racial segregation in one of two ways: by performing only for blacks, as William Carl decided to do, or by posing as foreigners and pretending not to be black.

Chapter 5

The Refined Entertainment of the Celebrated Armstrongs

By performing almost exclusively for black audiences, Professor J. Hartford Armstrong took a route similar to the one eventually taken by William Carl. Armstrong developed his act for church and school performances. He was the most successful black magician performing outside minstrel and vaudeville shows in the late nineteenth and early twentieth centuries.

John Hartford Armstrong was born in South Carolina around 1886. He was very light-complected and probably was of mixed race. According to the Armstrong legend, his father was a white man from Charleston; his black mother was named Erma Hartford.

Armstrong learned magic as an apprentice to a French magician who was touring the American South. By the time his mentor, whose name is not known, returned to France, the teenaged Armstrong could perform several magic tricks. With his brother,

Joseph, he began performing at black churches and schools throughout North and South Carolina. They billed themselves as Armstrong Brothers, Magicians, and were quite successful. Few other black magicians were entertaining black audiences at the turn of the century, so they didn't have a lot of competition.

After Joseph Armstrong lost interest in touring with a magic show, J. Hartford Armstrong teamed up briefly with a black comedian named Jordan. The act, billed as Armstrong and Jordan, did not last long either and eventually Armstrong decided to work as a solo performer. Even though his repertoire of magic was limited, his good looks and refined air appealed to his audiences.

With the money he made from performing, Armstrong purchased new tricks by mail. Occasionally he was hindered by the fact that most magicians were white. In 1907, he ordered from a magic dealer in Chicago a trick that involved making a handkerchief appear and disappear. When the trick arrived, Armstrong discovered that the key to the trick was a false finger—a pale pink false finger. Armstrong returned the trick, explaining that the color of the finger was too light for a black man to use. In time, Armstrong learned to adapt to such subtle prejudices— painting light-colored false fingers a darker color, for example.

J. Hartford Armstrong married around 1909. His wife, Mabel White, joined her husband's act as his assistant, and together they developed a full evening's entertainment of magic and illusions. Their stage presence and their genteel manner and attire were much admired. As time went on, the Armstrongs expanded their territory to include the entire East Coast and were particular favorites at segregated black colleges, such as Hampton Institute in Virginia. They also later found success working the black Lyceum and Chautauqua circuits.

The term *Lyceum* was coined by a white New Englander named Josiah Holbrook in 1826. He borrowed it from the place where the ancient Greek philosopher Aristotle lectured (the word *lyceum* comes from the Greek word for school). Holbrook's Lyceum was a small, private study group devoted to science, history, and art. The group met regularly and featured local speakers with some expertise or special interest in these subjects. Before long, Lyceum programs included both local speakers and visiting lecturers. Eventually, lecture bureaus arose for the purpose of booking speakers for Lyceum groups. Although music was introduced to Lyceum programs as early as 1830, musical groups were not commonplace until the middle 1870s.

By the late nineteenth century, magic acts were being included among Lyceum offerings. The white magician Edward Maro, who trained Alonzo Moore, was among the first to be represented by a Lyceum bureau. Lyceum entertainment was considered highbrow, as contrasted with the lowbrow entertainment of minstrelsy and vaudeville, and Lyceum magic was slower-paced. Many magicians, including Maro, played both Lyceum and vaudeville circuits, simply adapting their acts to the different formats.

Lyceums continued in popularity until they began to blend into the Chautauqua movement. The Chautauqua Summer Assembly was established in 1874 by Bishop John H. Vincent and Lewis Miller on the banks of Lake Chatauqua in upstate New York. It began as a training school for Sunday School teachers who attended to be inspired by lectures and Bible study. Entertainment was introduced to provide a break from the more serious offerings. Before long, other communities were establishing similar schools, keeping the term

Chautauqua. In many places, the Chautauqua took on aspects of the Lyceum and the programs were more cultural than religious.

By the early 1900s, a Chautauqua circuit had been established in Iowa and Mississippi, and soon other Chautauqua booking agencies were providing several days of concentrated lectures and entertainment to towns across the country. Circuit or tent Chautauquas often traveled long distances to far-flung communities. One of the most successful of these traveling tent shows was the Vawter Chautauqua. Its success was due in large measure to its imaginative operation. It was able to hit as many towns as possible in a short amount of time and thus to serve many audiences over the two months of summer.

David Price, author of *Magic: A Pictorial History of Conjurers in the Theater*, described the complex operations of the 1904 Vawter Chautauqua:

> The 1904 Vawter Chautauqua was a nine-day show. Therefore, it took ten tents to operate it. Imagine, if you will, ten tents set up in ten different towns. The first day's show comes to the first town, performs, and moves to the next town. The tent doesn't move. On the ninth day, nine tents are occupied, each with a different program. At the end of the day each unit moves to the next tent, which leaves the first tent empty. The chautauqua pulls up the tent and moves it to the eleventh town while the nine units are showing in each of nine towns. So each day there was only one tent to move, and each night the units all moved up one town. It caught on although it took the others eight years to organize.

A white magician named Edwin Brush performed on the Vawter Chautauqua's very first tour in 1904. So did a musical group called the Giant Colored Quartet. Most white Lyceum and Chautauqua shows, however, did not feature blacks. The prevailing antiblack attitudes in the country kept white stages white.

Blacks, however, formed their own Lyceum and Chautauqua circuits. These forms of entertainment appealed to the small but growing black middle class, which emphasized religion, education, and refined public amusements. Many in this group felt the need to distance themselves from the low-class entertainments with which whites associated blacks. Sadly, they also connected refinement with light-skinned complexions. The tan-skinned Professor J. Hartford Armstrong worked the black Lyceum and Chautauqua shows regularly. He was well respected in black communities and referred to by other black magicians as the King of the Colored Conjurors.

Armstrong apparently tried to crack the racial barrier only once and even then only in a modest and unusual way. According to Jim Magus, author of *Magical Heroes: The Lives and Legends of Great African American Magicians*, in 1914, in an effort to expand his audience, Armstrong sent out promotional brochures to the small number of schools in the Carolinas run by whites for American Indians. The mailing resulted in one booking, but it was a start. The Armstrongs traveled to the school expecting to perform their full evening show. To their surprise, when they arrived, the school's white principal told them the show had been cancelled. When the Armstrongs asked why, the principal said, "We did not realize from your publicity photograph that you were colored."

Armstrong never again tried to go outside the boundaries

of his own people. He also took steps to make sure that there would be no mistaking his racial heritage again. A window card he produced the following year made it clear who he and his wife were: "Coming—The Celebrated Armstrongs—Famous Colored Magicians—The Crowned Heads of Mystery—1889–1915."

In his promotional literature, Armstrong promised that he could duplicate at his comparatively modest venues the classic magic tricks that white magicians performed in big tent shows and on major stages. He presented the popular tricks of the time, including a sleight-of-hand trick called "The Miser's Dream" that seems to produce endless coins, and such illusions as the production of flowers and live doves.

Mabel White Armstrong died in 1914, shortly after giving birth to a daughter, who was named Ellen. After a time, Professor Armstrong remarried. Lily Mills Armstrong, who was the daughter of a Durham, North Carolina, doctor, joined her husband's act. An accomplished musician, she played the organ during the show and also assisted with her husband's mind-reading act. She would stand on the stage, blindfolded, facing the back of the stage area, while the professor went out among the audience. He would ask an audience member to hold up an object, and Lily Armstrong would accurately guess what it was. The Armstrongs would use the age-old trick of communicating with one another in coded words to perform the routine.

Little Ellen Armstrong grew up in show business. By the age of six, she was assisting her father as he presented his illusions. Early on, she displayed a talent for her parent's "psychic" line of work and even had her own portion of the show, doing mind-

Using Magic to
Teach Black History

From time to time, Professor J. Hartford Armstrong wove references to African-American history into his routines. For instance, he would include the story of Frederick Douglass in a version of the "Sand Frame" illusion. After displaying an empty picture frame, he would produce a photograph of Douglass. He would talk about Douglass's daring escape from slavery and his later career as an antislavery spokesman. He would then pass the photograph among the audience. Suddenly, the photograph would disappear from the hands of an unsuspecting audience member and magically reappear in a previously empty picture frame. Armstrong used this illusion to illustrate Douglass's escape from slavery.

reading. By the time she was in her teens, she had taken over another part of the show—drawing cartoons on a chalkboard in a routine that was known in the entertainment business as "chalk-talk."

She would doodle a cartoon on a blackboard and then, with a few more strokes of the chalk, change the original cartoon into something different. She would invite a member of the audience up on stage to do a doodle on the chalkboard, and then, with a few strokes, turn that doodle into a cartoon. She might

The Celebrated Armstrongs

NATIONAL COLORED **MAGICIANS Season 1920-21**

The Armstrongs were successful because they offered a program advertised as clean, clever, and classy to black churches and schools. On this National Colored Magicians program cover, Professor J. Hartford Armstrong is flanked by his daughter, Ellen, and his second wife (Ellen's stepmother), Lily.

Courtesy of Jim Magus

then add a few more strokes and turn the board upside down, revealing yet a different character.

On her father's death from heart failure in June 1939, Ellen Armstrong inherited his magic apparatus and carried on the show. She was probably the only female black magician touring the United States at the time. She continued to ply the same circuits her family had, focusing on black churches and schools up and down the East Coast. Although she married a North Carolina minister in the 1940s, she continued to use the Armstrong name on the stage.

In her early years on her own, Ellen Armstrong billed herself as Mistress of Modern Magic and featured the tricks and illusions that her father had performed. A poster for her act advertised such illusions as "The Miser's Dream" and "The Puzzling Parasol." The latter had been featured by her father as "The Mutilated Parasol." In the illusion, performed in pantomime, she began by opening and displaying with a twirl an ordinary umbrella, while her assistant displayed several silk scarves. The scarves were then placed in a cloth bag and the parasol was closed. Then the parasol was opened again, and magically, the scarves adorned the parasol. Adapting to the times, her "Sand Frame" illusion featured a photograph of the famed black boxer, Joe Louis, a hero in the black community after he knocked out the German fighter Max Schmeling in 1938.

As time went on, Ellen Armstrong focused more on the chalk-talk act that she had performed with her father as a teenager. Rather than a board and chalk, however, she began to use a large sketch pad and crayons so she could give her cartoons to children as souvenirs. She was so clever at producing humorous cartoons that by the 1960s she was emphasizing that

AN INVITATION TO MYSTERY BY

Ellen E. Armstrong
Mistress of
Modern Magic

ADMIT ONE

Ellen E. Armstrong carried on after her father's death in 1939, featuring chalk-talk cartooning. She was probably the only black female magician touring the United States in the mid-twentieth century.

Courtesy of Jim Magus

skill and billing herself as Cartoonist Extraordinary. Her promotional material from the time read: "Ellen E. Armstrong, in Her Modern Marvelous Matchless Merrymaking March through Mysteryland. The Act You Must See! If Laughing Hurts You . . . Stay at Home."

Ellen Armstrong retired in 1970 and spent her remaining years in a nursing home in Spartanburg, South Carolina, which had been her family's home base. In her time and to this day a black woman illusionist performing on her own is rare. So is a white woman magician performing alone. Most women in the field, black or white, are assistants or partners in magic acts.

Ellen Armstrong and her family found their niche performing for middle-class and working-class blacks who were not likely to attend minstrel or even most vaudeville shows. They took advantage of the Lyceum and Chautauqua movements that arose among blacks (as it had for whites) as a form of educational entertainment. In doing so, they were able to be themselves and not deny their race. Other black magicians working during this era felt forced to pretend they were foreign-born in order to succeed in American show business.

C h a p t e r

6

"Oriental" Conjurers

Nearly as rare as a black woman magician was a black magic act that could make a living performing exclusively for black audiences. The Armstrongs were unique for their time. During the years when black entertainers were barred from white stages, it was far more common for black magicians to pretend not to be black. They could accomplish this by claiming to be from a foreign land. Among the many stage names that William Carl used early in his career was the Creole Mahatma. The term *Creole* refers to a mixture and was often used to describe people in Louisiana, for example, who were of mixed African and French blood or African and Spanish blood. The term *mahatma*, which means great leader, is East Indian and reflects the growing American awareness of Asian Indian culture in the late 1800s. This created opportunities for black magicians to masquerade as "Hindus" and other exotic characters.

A phenomenon called "Orientalism" captured the imagination of the American general public, beginning around 1870 and lasting until about 1930. People in the United States were intrigued by travelers' tales and images of foreign lands with wondrous costumes and curious customs. The pictures conjured in their collective minds were of a seductive world of smoking hookahs, luscious fabrics, and jeweled riches. Artists (fine, commercial, and performing) brought these reveries to life— sometimes realistically, more often romantically. Americans watched movies that featured Rudolf Valentino as *The Sheik*, read Sherlock Holmes stories in which the famed British detective matched wits with mysterious Eastern villains, and listened to songs like Irving Berlin's "In My Harem."

American magicians seized on the general public's renewed fascination with East Indian snake charmers and street magicians. (Back in the early 1800s, Richard Potter's neighbors in New Hampshire had heard of such exotic characters and thought Potter might be a "Hindoo.") Dressed in rags and begging for their needs, they entertained passersby with mind-reading and feats such as walking on hot coals, lying on beds of nails, and suspending ropes in mid-air. As a group, they came to be called "Hindu Fakirs"; *fakir* being an Arabic word for India's intinerant "wonder-workers." Before long, many American-born magicians, conjurers, and spiritualists were adopting Indian-sounding stage names or claiming some relationship to Indian magic craft.

Among the white performers who masqueraded as mysterious magicians from the East was Jacob Houdini. In 1894, this brother of Harry Houdini was billing himself as "Houdini, Oriental Conjurer and Mysterious Juggler." Black magicians had

This artist's concept of a street show in India offers
some clues to the interest in Oriental magic on the part
of people in the United States. Black American
illusionists who were barred from performing because of
racial discrimination were welcomed when they
masqueraded as Hindus.

From The Illustrated History of Magic by Milbourne Christopher and
Maureen Christopher, courtesy of Maureen Christopher

even more reason to pass themselves off as of a nationality other than their own. They found that by posing as Hindus they could enjoy far greater opportunities in the entertainment field. White agents would book them into theaters that would ordinarily be closed to blacks. Also, no matter how dark their skin, if they could claim convincingly that they were foreigners, most segregation laws and customs in the United States did not apply to them. Black magicians posed as Hindus until well into the middle of the twentieth century.

ARTHUR DOWLING

Among the most successful black magicians to pass himself off as a Hindu Fakir was Arthur Dowling, who billed himself as Prince Jovedah de Rajah, the East Indian Psychic. His birth and early life are a mystery, and his life might not have been recorded by history at all if he were not the first black mentalist to succeed with his own show. Mentalists focus on mind-reading and pretending to use mental powers to move objects. A tall man, Dowling added to his height by wearing a blue turban. He also used a convincing foreign accent (it may not have been an East Indian accent, but then, not many among his audiences knew what a real East Indian accent sounded like anyway). He remained in character offstage as well, presenting himself as Indian royalty. He found that as a Hindu he could stay in whites-only hotels, eat in whites-only restaurants, and ride in the whites-only cars on trains. Of course, to convince people that he was of royal blood, he had to spend a lot of money.

Dowling was married to a white Canadian woman, who, billed as Princess Olga, assisted in his act. He worked with as many as five assistants. His act featured fortune-telling. A crystal ball was one of his standard props. In a typical performance, his assistants would hand out pencils and paper to audience members, who would write down questions. Prince Jovedah de Rajah would then astonish them by not only answering their questions but also revealing personal information that, it seemed, he could not have known except by mystical powers.

Nothing is known of Dowling's later life and career. According to legend, when he died in 1922 he was penniless.

The Code Act

Arthur Dowling accomplished his "mind-reading" feats by teaching his assistants to communicate with him in code. This code was exposed in *The Life and Mysteries of the Celebrated Dr. Q*, a 1921 book by a famous white mentalist who used the stage name Alexander. (In it, Alexander misspelled Dowling's name as "Prince Joedah Dah Radja.") There were code words for the subjects that people usually asked about: love, family, money, health. For example, one of Dowling's assistants would collect a written question from an audience member and, appearing to be friendly, ask the person to whisper to her how many children he had. The written question might be something like "Will my children be healthy in the coming year?" The assistant would communicate the question to Dowling using a code word that meant three children. Dowling would then answer, "Yes, I see good health for both you and your three children in the coming year." The audience member would gasp, not realizing that he had given out the very information he couldn't believe Dowling knew.

MARCELLUS R. CLARK

Another successful black magician who masqueraded as an Oriental conjurer was Marcellus R. Clark, who used the stage name Rhadolph Marcelliee. Born in Cambridge, Massachusetts, he became interested in magic when he met a black amateur magician named Henry Percival. Percival taught Clark a sleight-of-hand card trick called "The Pass." He also took him to a magic shop, where Clark could buy his own tricks. Clark did not dream of a professional career in magic, however, until he saw Alonzo Moore performing with Harvey's Minstrels at the Castle Square Theater in Boston. Moore's performance so inspired Clark that he decided to seek a career on the professional stage.

Clark was welcomed at black establishments and social gatherings, but he could not find much interest in his act on the part of white vaudeville booking agents. Then one evening he went to Lew Walker's Museum in Boston to see Professor Maharajah. This performer, whose real name was Wilmont Barclay, was masquerading as a Hindu hypnotist and escape artist. After seeing Barclay's act, Clark became determined to pass himself off as an Indian magician.

Billing himself as The Magician That Is Somewhat Different, Clark created a fictitious biography for his press releases. He claimed to have been born in the state of Madras in India, the son of a master of the occult sciences, and to have traveled to the United States from England. After he married in New York in the 1920s, his wife, Alma, assisted him and was billed as Princess Almasjid Marcelliee.

As a Hindu mentalist and escape artist, Clark was able to get

As Marcelliee, Marcellus R. Clark was a highly successful
Oriental conjurer. When that type of magician went out
of fashion, he developed a faith-healing program and
became Doctor Marcelliee.

Courtesy of Jim Magus

work here and there. In the time-honored tradition of magicians, he befriended other magicians along the way and learned new tricks from them. In the decade following 1910, a number of West Indian magicians and mentalists toured the United States. Wilmont Barclay, aka Professor Maharajah, the first black magician Clark ever saw, was probably West Indian. Clark made friends with several of them. One, a magician from the Virgin Islands named Henry Perry, worked for a time as his assistant.

Another West Indian performer Clark knew was Professor J. T. Boston, who had been born in Haiti and who presented an act that included trained dogs, voodoo spells, and a clever piece called the "Hobie Stick" act. The hobie stick was made of wood, and after passing it around for examination Boston would set it afire. He then chanted to it in a strange tongue and appeared to cause the stick to dance in the air. After seeing Boston perform, Clark introduced himself and asked how he did the "Hobie Stick" trick. Boston made Clark promise not to use the trick in his own act as long as Boston was still performing it. On securing that promise, he taught Clark the secret. Clark kept his promise and used the trick only after Boston died in 1912.

In 1919, Clark joined a show with Alfonso Hanbin. Hanbin was a native of Barbados in the British West Indies, and had been featured with the Barnum & Bailey Circus in 1911 and 1912. He billed himself as The Human Ostrich and specialized in eating glass, tacks, and other dangerous items.

Still another West Indian acquaintance of Clark's used the stage name Professor Lawrence. When Clark met him in Boston in 1919, he was wearing a British uniform, having served in the British army during World War I. But in civilian life he had been a magician and ventriloquist. After World War

I, he moved from his native Jamaica to the United States and settled in Philadelphia. Clark kept in touch with Professor Lawrence until Lawrence died in 1955.

Over the years, Clark performed in a variety of venues in many different shows. He teamed up with a white couple, Alfonso Blake and his wife, whose escape routine was called "Enigma." He opened the show with magic and ventriloquism, after which the Blakes escaped from handcuffs, chains, and straitjackets. Around 1926, he performed with Professor Maharajah in a show at Starlight Park in the Bronx in New York City. The two then joined a carnival and went on a twenty-five-week road tour. After that tour ended, Clark and his wife and Professor Maharajah played in various New York City theaters with a company that totaled eight people. The Clarks, billing themselves as "Oriental Exponents of the Art of Mental Telepathy," did a mentalist act, while Professor Maharajah performed various illusions and climaxed the show by escaping from a milk can.

Clark enjoyed one of the longest careers among African-American magicians. In the 1930s, he and his wife developed a faith-healing program. As Doctor and Madame Marcelliee they did mind-reading and lectured on the Bible. They performed at black churches and often invited a local minister to share the program with them.

At some point, Alma Clark retired from the entertainment business, and Marcellus Clark continued as a solo act. In *Magical Heroes: The Lives and Legends of Great African American Magicians*, Jim Magus reported that Clark was the first black magician to perform at an International Brotherhood of Magicians convention—in Philadelphia in 1952. Relating a story he heard, Magus said that Clark was paid nothing but cab fare and that his name was not even on the program. His mere appearance in the show caused a stir because he was black.

Clark was still performing in the late 1960s and still promoting himself in brochures of his own creation. Apparently, he was also still embroidering his life story. A brochure he produced in 1968, entitled "Around the World by Magic," claimed that he had toured Europe, although no official record of that trip exists. Marcellus R. Clark died in 1971.

CLARENCE HUNTER

Among other African-American magicians who chose to pose as "Hindus" in order to get work was Clarence Hunter. Born in Pittsburgh, Pennsylvania, on October 7, 1920, Hunter began performing in 1940. When club owners objected to booking a black performer, he transformed himself into a "Hindu." He wore a turban and took the stage name Chandu the Magician from a 1932 movie of the same title. His first work was in carnivals, where he chose tricks that befitted a Hindu sorcerer— fire-eating and walking on broken class. By the early 1940s, he had his own radio show in Pittsburgh, a fifteen-minute daily show that brought him local renown and bookings in nightclubs and theaters.

By the late 1940s, he was touring the East Coast. Horror movies had become all the rage by this time, and Hunter found work at theaters, performing a brief midnight magic show before the screening of horror films.

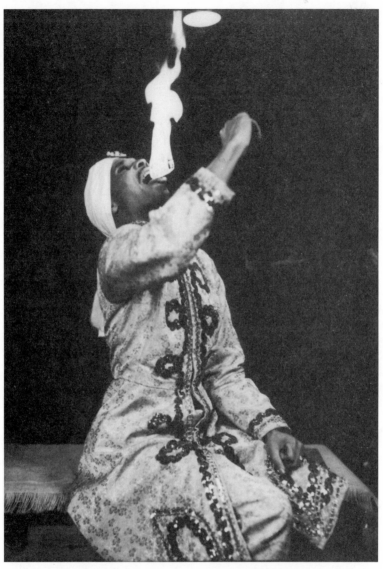

Clarence "Chandu" Hunter was another Oriental conjurer
who was quite successful. His specialty was fire-eating.
He boasted: "I bathe, eat and play in fire."

Courtesy of Jim Magus

The Human Cigarette Lighter

Hunter's most famous trick was called "The Human Cigarette Lighter." He blew flames through a metal tube to light the cigarette of an audience volunteer. His secret was to hide a small ball of absorbent cotton, soaked with high-test gasoline, in his mouth. Inserting the metal tube in his mouth, he would exhale across the cotton into the tube, light the end of the tube, and keep it burning as long as he kept blowing.

Hunter relocated to San Francisco, California, around 1950. He found a ready audience on the West Coast for his fire-eating act, and got bookings at hotels. The media soon discovered him, and he performed on NBC-TV's *Breakfast in Hollywood* show in 1954 and appeared as an extra in several Hollywood films.

"I bathe, eat and play in fire," he boasted to interviewers. "I play with hot lead in my mouth, take baths in gasoline and set myself on fire. I can step in a red-hot oven and roast a pound of meat in it but I will emerge as cool as ice." Shaving with an acetylene blowtorch was one of his specialties. So was fire-walking in a box of broken bottles soaked with burning gasoline. The trick of stomping out the fire with his bare feet took him three months to perfect. Hunter suffered third-degree burns on several occasions. Once, he even set his own face on fire.

In 1957, Hunter was performing in a nightclub in Detroit

when a traumatic incident occurred that he would never discuss, other than to describe it as an instance of racism. Perhaps as a result of this incident, he changed the direction of his life. He quit acting the part of a Hindu. He moved to Cleveland, Ohio, married, and went to work as a building maintenance man at a YMCA branch. He also worked as a photographer for the Cleveland Air Show and for attorneys representing accident victims. Under his own name, Clarence Hunter, he continued to perform magic, including his fire-eating act, at schools, nightclubs, and parties, and also worked trade shows. In addition, he taught magic with a fellow magician named Bob Wheeler, whom he had met at Snyder's Magic Shop in Cleveland. A young man named Jack Vaughn was one of his students. Vaughn later became famous as the magician Goldfinger. Another student was Arsenio Hall, who started his show-business career doing magic tricks but later switched to comedy and hosted a long-running late-night television talk show.

Clarence "Chandu" Hunter retired from maintenance work in 1990, at the age of 70. He continued performing magic at hospitals and benefits until cancer forced him to curtail even those activities. He died in January 1993.

Hunter was probably the last of the well-known Hindu Fakirs. By the time he quit performing as an East Indian mystic, the racial climate in the United States had undergone a radical change. Federal laws had ended legal segregation, and although blacks still met with racial barriers, they no longer felt the need to pose as members of another race to get work.

ARSENIO

AWARD WINNING

MAGICIAN & ILLUSIONIST

THE MYSTIC RINGS

MAGIC ON WINGS

BOOKINGS FOR ALL AFFAIRS

PHONE 831-3487

Arsenio Hall was one of Chandu Hunter's students. He
started his show-business career doing magic tricks but
later switched to comedy and hosted a long-running
late-night television talk show.

Courtesy of Jim Magus

Chapter 7

Black Herman: "Once in Every Seven Years"

Barred by prejudice from white entertainment stages, many black magicians plied their trade in black communities across the country during the first decades of the twentieth century. Their audiences were appreciative, but of modest means, and the sponsors of these shows were rarely able to pay a substantial fee to the entertainers. As a result, most black magicians, even those who were successful, never made much money. Black Herman was an exception. He possessed the unique combination of charisma and financial shrewdness to make a fortune serving (or exploiting, depending on one's opinion) the black community.

Black Herman was born Benjamin Rucker in Amherst, Virginia, in 1892. Little is known of his early years. He had a brother named Andrew. He attended school briefly in Lynchburg, Virginia, then moved back to Amherst, where he stayed five years. He was working in a lunchroom in Amherst when he met a black traveling salesman. The man called himself Prince Herman and peddled a "special health tonic" to black communities. Part of the entertainment Prince Herman presented to attract customers was a card trick that magicians call a "Si Stebbins routine," named after a well-known magician. No matter how well a pack of cards was shuffled, or who shuffled it, Prince Herman knew the location of every card in the deck.

No one was more fascinated with the trick than young Benjamin Rucker, and he asked Prince Herman to teach him the routine. The two became friends, and, according to legend, on Rucker's sixteenth birthday Prince Herman offered him a job as his assistant.

Rucker eagerly assented, and for the next year or so he acted as chauffeur, ticket seller, packer and unpacker, and general go-fer for Prince Herman. All the while, he watched and listened and learned the secrets of Prince Herman's magic tricks. When Prince Herman died in 1909, young Rucker had learned enough to follow in his mentor's footsteps.

Rucker took the stage name Black Herman. He continued to sell health tonic, having learned from Prince Herman how to mix up an exotic-tasting brew from simple and easily available ingredients. Calling his elixir "Herman's Wonderful Body Tonic," he would attract a crowd by setting up a large iron pot over a bonfire and cooking up a batch of tonic on the spot. He was his own best advertisement for his brew, for he was tall and well built, and made a point of dressing expensively. It would not have done for a skinny weakling to have peddled health tonic, or for a man dressed in rags to have trumpeted his brew as a secret of success. He would urge spectators to toss a dime into the iron pot for good luck.

Early in his independent career, Rucker realized that the image he projected was the key to success. Aiming for greater respectability, for a time he billed himself as Professor Black Herman, a Bachelor of Divinity, and paid local ministers to appear with him. He added faith-healing to his repertoire and sprinkled his presentation with fortune-telling, claiming that his knowledge was grounded in Christian faith but hinting at a knowledge of voodoo and other occult practices.

Aware that his fortune-telling was more popular than his elixir, Rucker soon began to emphasize it, getting around local laws that forbade fortune-telling for pay by offering a reading as a free bonus if someone bought his tonic. He became a master at "cold-reading," using the same skills as Arthur Dowling (Prince Jovedah de Rajah), for example, to find out information from people and then give it back to them. People were fooled into believing that he had the psychic ability to see into their lives. Like Dowling, he had help from other people. He would often send his brother, Andrew, and his chief assistant, Washington Reeves, ahead to gather information about the community in which they would be performing. The two men would listen to town gossip, note local names and events, and even visit cemeteries to get names and dates from tombstones. They then shared the information they had gathered with Rucker, who would present the information as having come to him by mystical means.

Once he began to focus on mind-reading, Black Herman's popularity increased greatly. He was able to expand his troupe and hire attractive female assistants. Among them was Madame Debora Sapphirra, who was billed in his program as a mentalist and adviser.

Rucker now added a number of crowd-pleasing magic tricks to his show. These classic magic tricks included the "Sawing the Lady in Half" illusion and a "Sword Cabinet" trick. In the first, he placed one of his female assistants in a box. He would then appear to saw her in half and then magically make her whole again. In the second, the "Sword Cabinet" trick, he would place one of his assistants in a box and appear to thrust swords into it (and into her body). When the box was opened, she would step out unharmed. He also introduced what is called the "Asrah Levitation" illusion, in which he would put one of his assistants into a trance and lay her down on a couch. Covering her body with a cloth, he would appear to cause the cloth-covered body to rise several feet into the air.

Seeing audience responses to his tricks, Rucker decided to write a how-to magic book. Black Herman's *Easy Pocket Tricks That You Can Do* went through at least fourteen editions (meaning that it was republished at least thirteen times) and was still being published in New York in the 1930s. No wonder. The book promised to provide the reader with "a two hour's performance with one hour's practice."

By the early 1920s, Black Herman was famous throughout the Midwest. He and his wife, Eva, and their three children lived in a large apartment in Chicago, where many southern blacks had migrated at the time of World War I. The hub of middle America, Chicago was accessible via railroad or automobile to most of the major Midwest cities. The city's large black population included a solid middle class, who could afford to pay admission to his large presentations, as well as a substantial working class who believed they would never get anywhere without some good luck. They eagerly sought out Black Her-

Black Herman was an entrepreneur, turning his fame as a mentalist into a veritable family business, publishing books, offering mail-order magic courses, selling health tonic, and even marketing a line of beauty products.

Courtesy of Jim Magus

man to give them lucky numbers and other devices to bring good fortune.

Rucker was dissatisfied with his success in Chicago and set his sights on New York City, the largest American city and the one with perhaps the greatest opportunities for entertainers. When he got the chance to do a big show there, he saw it as an occasion to take the city by storm.

He secured a month-long booking at Liberty Hall, the head-quarters of Marcus Garvey's Universal Negro Improvement Association (UNIA). Born in Jamaica, Garvey (1887–1940) had spent time in London, where he had become interested in African history and black nationalism. His interests led him to establish the UNIA to promote the spirit of racial pride by emphasizing the greatness of the African heritage and to foster worldwide unity among all blacks. In 1916, Garvey immigrated to New York City, where he opened a branch of the UNIA in Harlem, which was fast becoming the "black capital of the world."

As in Chicago, many southern blacks had migrated to New York City during and after World War I, seeking freedom from brutal segregation in the South and attracted by the burgeoning industries in the North. At about the same time, plans for extending the elevated railroad lines from downtown New York City northward to Harlem had spurred a building boom, which went bust after the combined effects of overspeculation in building and delays in completion of the rail lines. Black realtors saw an opportunity to buy up Harlem buildings and rent them to blacks, and blacks were eager to escape from the overcrowded slums of the Tenderloin and San Juan Hill neighborhoods in the West 50s and 60s. By the early 1920s, Harlem had a large concentration of blacks of all economic levels. Black New Yorkers responded to Garvey's message and joined the UNIA in droves, buying copies of his newspaper, *Negro World*; attending the UNIA's annual conventions; and buying stock in his steamship company, the Black Star Line. It was Garvey's intention that the ships of the Black Star Line would transport American blacks to Africa, where they would establish an autonomous black state and pursue their own culture and civilization free from the domination of whites. His emphasis on African-tinged ceremonial trappings and honorifics, his organizational skills, and his brilliant oratory attracted millions of followers across the United States. Because of his power, he was soon perceived as a threat by American authorities. Convicted of mail fraud in connection with the sale of stock in the Black Star Line, he was imprisoned in 1925 and deported to Jamaica two years later. Once he was forced to leave New York, Garvey's influence waned. Although his American followers attempted to keep his movement alive in his absence, they were unsuccessful.

When Benjamin Rucker arrived in New York, Garvey was at the height of his influence, and Liberty Hall was the major arena for blacks to come together on the East Coast. According to Black Herman's autobiography, written in the third person, "He secured a month's engagement in Liberty Hall, the headquarters of Garvey's organization, an immense structure, which covers a five acre lot, and comfortably seats four thousand people. Herman did what no other Negro in Harlem has ever done, except Marcus Garvey. He packed Liberty Hall from platform to door for sixty nights. Some nights hundreds of people were turned away."

From then on, Rucker was often invited to perform at major entertainment events, such as the time in the summer of 1923 when he appeared at the Independence Day Jubilee and Aviation Carnival and Athletic Meet in Hasbrouck Heights, New Jersey. The athletic events included track races, boxing, baseball, tennis, cricket, a potato race (possibly in potato sacks), and a three-legged race. There was also a midway with carnival booths and rides. A featured performer at the event was Lieutenant Herbert Julian, the renowned African-American pilot. He was famous for stunt flying and parachuting. Rucker seized the opportunity to use Julian to bring attention to his "Buried Alive" stunt. This trick had been taught to him by Wilmont Barclay, aka Professor Maharajah, whom he had met at a fair in San Francisco (the same Professor Maharajah who inspired Marcellus Clark to become a magician). He sent out a press release before the festival announcing that he would bury a woman under six feet of earth at 11:00 A.M. on the day of the festival and then unearth her at 4:45 P.M. To make the unearthing even more exciting, he had Julian parachute from his airplane down onto the burial spot. Then he dramatically freed the woman from her grave.

Deciding to make his headquarters in New York City, Rucker purchased a three-story townhouse at 119 West 136th Street in Harlem. He spared no expense in furnishing the house. He had a telephone installed on each floor—an almost unheard-of luxury at the time. He described its furnishings in his autobiography: "Beautiful pictures were painted on the walls and ceilings. . . . A double set of electric lights was installed. A radio, piano, elegant rugs, and valuable antiques were placed in the home. A speedwagon, two Studebaker cars, and a roadster were purchased. Professor Herman put money into circulation."

Black Herman on His Liberty Hall Performance

In his autobiography, Black Herman recounted his mind-reading feats at Liberty Hall in New York City:

"His assistants passed out slips of paper to members of the audience, and from the stage, Herman answered a great variety of questions. He advised men and women whether to hold their jobs, or to move to fresh fields and pastures new. . . . He brought together estranged couples, and husbands and wives who had separated. Men and women asked: 'What manner of man is this? Where does black Herman get his wonderful knowledge and marvelous dexterity? He is a real wizard, a super-master of the "BLACK ART."' . . . The fame of his New York performance in Liberty Hall spread far and wide, and soon he became the man of the hour as an entertainer."

One room in the house was specially furnished. The walls were painted black and hung with African masks carved in frightening grimaces. It featured an altar decorated with voodoo symbols and a human skull surrounded by candles. Near the altar, African drums rigged to play by themselves completed the atmosphere of black magic.

Behind the house, a special garden was laid out for the purpose of growing fresh ingredients for the health tonic, the production and marketing of which Andrew Rucker was in charge. Benjamin Rucker's brother also oversaw the Black Herman Mail Order Course of Graduated Lessons in the Art of Magic.

In addition to health tonic, Rucker marketed beauty products. His wife, Eva, was in charge of the Beauty Department. The couple had three children, two daughters and a son, when they moved to Harlem. Subsequently, they had another daughter, Louise, whom Rucker claimed to have produced from a pocket handkerchief from the air.

When he was not on tour, Rucker presided over salons in his Harlem home to which wealthy and cultured black Harlemites were invited. Among these stars of Harlem society was A'lelia Walker, daughter of Madame C. J. Walker, whose hair-care products had made her the first self-made American woman millionaire, black or white. A'lelia Walker had her own lavish home in Harlem. Rucker also held private readings. It was said that he employed two secretaries just to take fortune-telling appointments.

During this time the "Numbers" was a major illegal gambling racket in Harlem. Like a lottery, it involved betting money on a certain combination of numbers. At the end of the day, when the racing results were reported from a local track, the racetrack scores provided the winning combination. Many poor Harlemites played the Numbers because the bets could be as small as a quarter. The thought rarely occurred to them that the mathematical odds against winning were huge. Rather, Numbers players firmly believed that "lucky numbers" came to them in dreams, or were associated with events that happened to them. Lucky Number Dream Books and other devices for choosing winning numbers were in great demand. Much of Black Herman's fortune-telling business focused on providing lucky numbers to his clients.

According to a legend probably made up by Rucker himself, the white mobsters who controlled the Numbers racket in Harlem became concerned that he was giving out too many winning numbers. Having too many winners cut into their profits. One day, two thugs who worked for Dutch Schultz and Joey Rao, the top Numbers controllers in Harlem, arrived at Black Herman's home to threaten him with bodily harm unless he stopped giving out winning numbers. Far from being intimidated, Black Herman used the occasion to frighten the gangsters.

Ushering the men into his special voodoo chamber, Black Herman used all the tricks in his repertoire to scare them thoroughly. He caused the drums to pound, called on voodoo spirits to curse them, and presented them with a voodoo doll stuck with a pin. His assistant, Washington Reeves, gained entry to the hotel rooms where Joey Rao's gang resided. Reeves bribed one of the hotel maids to rig the shower head in one of the gangster's bathrooms so that it would shower red paint. According to the legend, the hapless hood who took the first shower in that bathroom suffered a nervous breakdown and spent the rest of his life in a mental institution.

Black Herman took the lucky number seven as part of his mystique. He would announce that he came "once in every seven years." A disgruntled former assistant complained that seven years was how long it took for the people he had cheated to forgive him. At one point after he had moved to New York, he was arrested on charges of fortune-telling for money and spent a

For this portrait photograph, Black Herman dressed in a
formal style that befitted his success. In sporting a ribbon
across his chest, he may have been influenced by Marcus
Garvey, who affected a similar ribbon. It was first published
with the caption: "The Original Black Herman, the world
famous magician, master of Legerdemain, holds in his hand
the paper containing all of the magic secrets which have
been hidden for centuries."

Courtesy of Jim Magus

short time in Sing Sing prison in Ossining, New York. On his release, he turned the situation to his advantage. He announced in press releases that he had been arrested seven times and seven times walked out of his cell. The authorities, his press releases claimed, had finally freed him because the iron bars could not hold him.

Although Black Herman claimed to have toured extensively in the United States, it is unlikely that he ventured very far into the South. A successful black man—especially a self-promoter like Benjamin Rucker—would not have been welcome there. In fact, his life would have been in danger from whites who resented his refusal to stay in his "place." Not only southern whites felt that way; many northern whites did as well. Rucker remained in the black community, where he was both accepted and envied. Focusing on lucky numbers in his acts and on the various businesses he ran out of his home, he did not have to worry about keeping current with his magic tricks. When the stock market crashed in October 1929, ushering in the Great Depression, his career and his businesses were largely unaffected. The Depression caused millions of people to lose their jobs and was particularly hard on the working-class black people who made up his most loyal audience. In such a time of severe financial hardship, people needed the hope that a fortune-teller could offer. They also sought out entertainment as a relief from the harsh realities of daily life.

For his 1933 tour, Rucker decided he needed a new trick to capture the imagination of his audiences. He decided to adapt his "Woman Buried Alive" trick and instead bury himself. Press releases announced the trick: "Come see Black Herman in his Private Graveyard. He will be buried, and return from the grave to perform an astonishing show of magic and good fortune. Yes, even Death will not stop the Great Black Herman."

Several days before each stop on the tour, Black Herman's front men would arrange to convert a plot of ground near the theater into a cemetery. Interested spectators were charged five cents to view the body of the magician in a coffin next to a six-foot deep grave. Someone would be invited to feel Herman's wrist for a pulse and would feel none. Herman, using a balled handkerchief in his armpit to artificially stop his pulse, would appear to be dead. The coffin was nailed shut and lowered into the grave, which was then filled with soil. The crowd was invited to return in several days to witness Black Herman's remarkable return from the dead.

Rucker was far too busy, though, to remain lying in the grave for several days. By way of a secret passage, he left the coffin, and in disguise, traveled on to his next tour stop to set up his publicity machine there.

On the appointed day, he would return to the private graveyard and slip back into the coffin. On the evening of the show, the coffin would be dug up with great ceremony, the lid would be pried off, and Black Herman would emerge from the coffin. The amazed crowd would follow him to the theater.

In April 1934, while performing onstage at the Old Palace Theater in Louisville, Kentucky, Benjamin Rucker suddenly collapsed. If the birth date in his "life story" can be believed, he was only forty-two years old. A doctor in the audience tried to revive him but was unsuccessful. The cause of death was probably a heart attack but was listed officially as "acute indigestion." The audience, certain that this was just another of Herman's tricks, waited patiently for him to miraculously return to life.

Even after the body was delivered to a local funeral home, crowds of people came to witness his resurrection. Herman's longtime assistant and friend, Washington Reeves, ever the showman, decided to take advantage of the situation. He charged ten cents for the opportunity to view the body of the great Black Herman.

Eventually, Herman's body was taken to a railroad station, where it was shipped home to his family in Harlem. The funeral was held at Mother A.M.E. Zion Church on West 137th Street in Harlem; his body was buried in Woodlawn Cemetery in the Bronx.

The persistent notion that Black Herman was not really dead fueled efforts by several black magicians to impersonate him. Five years after his death, magicians were billing themselves as Black Herman. Among them was his former assistant and friend, Washington Reeves, who performed under the stage name The Original Black Herman. Others, who had less nerve, exploited his fame by attaching themselves to his legend. A magician named Warren Hugo performed in the South as Black Herman the Second. Others called themselves Black Herman, Jr.

Black Herman never returned, but his legend lived on. Dead or alive, he remains the most famous black magician of the early twentieth century. He was also the most financially successful.

8

Fetaque Sanders: From Discrimination to Equal Rights

In 1933, a year before Black Herman died, Fetaque Sanders began his professional career as a magician. He never achieved Black Herman's financial success, but he reached a wider and more diverse audience. Benjamin Rucker probably never performed on a white stage. Fetaque Sanders's career, however, bridged the era of discrimination and the era of equal rights for blacks. While most of his work was before black audiences, he occasionally performed for whites. He influenced many younger people, who carry on his legacy in a much more welcoming racial atmosphere.

Sanders was born on May 12, 1915, in Nashville, Tennessee, the son of William N. and Minnie Johnson Sanders. Other children had been born to the Sanderses, but they had died in infancy; Fetaque was the only one to survive. Fetaque (pronounced "Fee-take") was his given name, and when he embarked on a career as a professional magician, there was no need to create a more elaborate stage name.

William Sanders had been born to poor sharecroppers in Newberry, South Carolina. He had worked his way through Benedict College in Columbia, South Carolina, and also attended Hampton Institute, an all-black college in Virginia, graduating in 1911. After graduation, he married Minnie Johnson, and the couple moved to Nashville, Tennessee, where there was a substantial black community. Working as an insurance salesman, William Sanders came to know a large number of people in that community. He helped establish the first YMCA for blacks in the city. Minnie Johnson Sanders was also active in civic causes and in the First Baptist Church of Capital Hill.

Fetaque was born when the couple were in their thirties. He had a comfortable childhood, far different from that of his father. His family could afford the admission prices at local theaters. From an early age he enjoyed attending shows at a theater for blacks in Nashville, the Bijou Theatre. He also managed to gain admittance to the white theaters by offering to put up advertising handbills in exchange for a free ticket. He sat in the balcony area reserved for blacks, but he didn't care where he sat, so long as he was able to see the show.

His introduction to magic came when he was visiting his mother's parents in Marion, South Carolina. A black magician called "Tricky Sam" Tatum was performing there, and nine-year-old Fetaque volunteered to participate in one of Tatum's tricks. Up on stage, Tatum miraculously produced a silver dollar from Sanders's ear, another from his tongue, another from his pocket. In this classic sleight-of-hand trick called the "Miser's Dream," a seemingly endless supply of coins is produced. Sanders was fascinated. He could not figure out how Tatum had done the trick. From then on, he was hooked on magic.

Back home, Sanders traded some of his toys for a friend's twenty-five-cent magic set and began to practice the tricks in it. When he had mastered the tricks, he decided to put on his own magic show. He put up signs in the neighborhood and had a sizable audience for his debut show in a local coal house. He charged two cents admission. In that first show, Sanders featured his version of the "Multiplying Billiard Balls" trick. Because his hands were too small to hold more than one billiard ball, he used cherries instead. He began the routine holding one cherry between his thumb and forefinger, then miraculously produced a second cherry between his forefinger and middle finger, then another between his middle finger and ring finger, and so on. Audience response to that first show was so enthusiastic that Sanders began learning more tricks. He discovered that the Nashville public library had books on magic, as well as copies of the magazine *Science and Invention*, which regularly carried articles on magic tricks. He also began to visit Dodson's magic shop, whose proprietor took an interest in the youngster and urged him to practice showmanship as well as magic tricks.

Sanders's parents had good-naturedly accepted their son's interest in magic when it seemed a harmless diversion. They started to worry when they realized he was becoming obsessed with the art. His father had plans for Fetaque to become a doctor or a lawyer. To middle-class blacks like his parents, entertainers were low-class. Although Fetaque loved and respected his parents, he was determined to become a professional magician and took to hiding his preoccupation from them. He would skip school in order to visit Dodson's magic shop, and would pretend that his Sunday afternoons at the public library were for the purpose of his school studies rather than his studies in magic. He also continued to buy or work his way into any show that came through town, especially if there was a magic act in it. In this way he managed to see just about every great magician who performed in Nashville.

By the time he was in his early twenties, Sanders felt he was ready to turn professional. Even his parents had come around to his way of thinking. Having seen him perform, they realized he had a true gift. With their blessing, he set off for Chicago in the spring of 1933 to audition for a part in a stage show that would be performed at the World's Fair to be held that summer. After several unsuccessful auditions, he managed to impress the manager of the Enchanted Island Theater. His career as a professional entertainer was launched, although not without some difficulty.

At his very first appearance on the stage of the Enchanted Island Theater, Sanders decided to delight his audience with a trick he called "Cutting a Girl in Two with Ropes." He solicited a volunteer from the audience and then fastened two pieces of rope around her waist. He commanded his audience to watch closely as he tugged at one of the ropes, for he would cut the girl in two. He pulled at one of the ropes, only to discover that he had mistied them and neither would budge. Rather than getting flustered, Sanders showed the instincts of a true showman when he turned to the audience and said "Suppose we try another trick . . ."

The crowd laughed, and Sanders finished the rest of the show without further mishap. By the end of his act the manager of the theater had offered him a two-week booking.

Sanders's successful engagement at the Chicago World's Fair led to performances in other cities and towns. While maintaining an ambitious performance schedule, he took his father's advice to get an education. He returned to Nashville and in the fall enrolled at Tennessee A&I (Agricultural and Industrial) State College. He took courses in business and advertising. Keenly aware that a professional entertainer needed to know how to market himself, he learned all he could about self-promotion.

On weekends and during school vacations, Sanders performed at local black schools and churches. On one occasion, he joined up with the Mighty Haag Circus, which was in town. When he approached the manager about a job, he was told there were only two roles for colored performers—blackface minstrel or Arabian magician. Sanders was unhappy about the choice, but dutifully went to the wardrobe tent to claim a turban and "Arab" costume. He billed himself as Feta Sajii and rode a camel in the circus street parade that preceded the show.

While with the Mighty Haag Circus, Sanders discovered the Punch and Judy puppet show, which has its roots in Italian comedy and traveled to England by way of France in the seventeenth century. Seeing how audiences responded to the slapstick comedy of the show, he determined to add puppetry to his repertoire. After he finished his classes at Tennessee State in the spring of 1938, he bought a second-hand set of Punch and Judy figures and practiced manipulating the puppets. He also designed and built a cabinet for their performance.

Sanders did a variety act. In addition to puppetry, he performed impressions of well-known figures, white and black. Comedian Jack Benny and actor James Cagney were among his best imitations. One of his funniest skits was his impression of

NOW FEATURING
The Friendliest **GHOST** Ever
To Leave The Graveyard!!
FUN for EVERYONE
will be
HERE

To better publicize his one-man variety show, Sanders took
courses in advertising at Tennessee State College, a black
college in Nashville. He advised younger performers
to concentrate as much on promotion as on
their performances.

Courtesy of Dave Price

The Ballad of
the Red-Headed Queen

One of Fetaque Sanders's most popular original routines was "The Ballad of the Red-Headed Queen." Sanders used three oversized playing cards, a King, a Queen, and a Deuce. Speaking in rhyme with a Shakespearean accent, he reversed the cards, showing that the back of the Queen card was blue, while the other two cards were red. Turning the cards frontward again, Sanders explained that the King "raised the Deuce" because the Queen had dyed her hair red and he was going to fight with her. He then turned the cards around again to show their backs, and surprisingly, the back of the Queen card was now red. Sometimes he incorporated the boxing star Joe Louis into the routine. In this version, when he turned the Queen card around, the back contained a picture of Louis. The King, explained Sanders, decided not to fight the Queen after all.

the black comedian Stepin Fetchit, who'd become famous playing the stereotypical lazy black. Sanders called his impression of Stepin Fetchit the "World's Laziest Magician." Sanders also did a fine impression of boxing star Joe Louis, at the time the most revered man among African Americans.

With his one-man variety show, Sanders played the black

school circuit. He put what he had learned in advertising courses at Tennessee State to good use marketing his show. He obtained a directory of the black schools in Tennessee and a map of the state and embarked on a carefully thought out promotional campaign. First, he sent promotional material to each school. Then, he personally visited each principal to explain how his shows could be used as school fundraisers. Securing a booking, he then visited the local newspaper, did a few tricks for the editor, and thus got the paper to run an article about his upcoming show. He also made a practice of visiting a school assembly the afternoon before the show and doing a preview, to ensure that the students would attend the evening performance with their families.

In a letter to the *Nashville Banner* in 1991, Maxine Thurman-Caruth recalled seeing Sanders perform at her elementary school in Nashville in the late 1930s: "We were reared to call all adults Mr. or Mrs., except for Fetaque Sanders. We were allowed to call him by his full name—not Mr. Sanders, and not Fetaque. To us, a visit from Fetaque Sanders to our school was a treat equal to Santa Claus. He was so giving, so caring, so funny and so good. Such stimulation for our imagination!"

Sanders was a born teacher as well as an entertainer. Although he would not reveal how he did his tricks, he always tried to relate his tricks to real life. He published a booklet on magic, *Ten Easy Trix That You Can Do*. He was more interested, however, in sharing what he had learned about self-promotion. *Sell Your Act with Posters* and *Sell Your Act with Letters* were two of his how-to publications.

Although he didn't get rich performing for school audiences, Sanders made enough money to buy a trailer, which enabled him to travel farther afield. "Colored folks were proud of me to have a trailer and going places," he later remarked. "We went where we wanted but, of course, in that social climate you had to be smart and make the best of the situation." He was referring, of course, to the segregation he encountered on the road. He was fortunate to own a trailer and not have to worry about being turned away at segregated hotels.

In January 1939, Sanders appeared at the Society for the Study of Negro History in Washington, D.C. The nation's capital had a large black middle class and many opportunities for black performers. He soon relocated to the District of Columbia.

Fetaque Sanders married after he moved to Washington, D.C. His wife, Irene Kennedy, had been a volunteer from the audience at one of his shows. (He was in the habit of choosing good-looking women volunteers, and he had a reputation as a ladies' man—in fact, one of his fellow performers had dubbed him Fe-Take the Female Taker.) After completing a routine with his beautiful volunteer, Sanders had invited her to dinner after the show. She accepted, and a romance developed from there. They were married in 1942. Irene joined her husband's show as his onstage assistant, and the two performed on Broadway in New York City for the first time in early May 1943. *Magic on Broadway* at the New York Times Hall was a gala event directed by Orson Welles, a young and talented director. Welles would later make history with a radio show entitled "War of the Worlds" that seemed so real to its listeners that the country nearly went into a panic. *Magic on Broadway* featured John Mulholland, Ned Rutledge, Count Artell and Ann Lorey, Professor Dum Bunny and Company, and several other white magicians and troupes. Sanders was the only black on the program.

The United States had entered World War II after Japan bombed the U.S. Navy fleet at Pearl Harbor, in Hawaii, on December 7, 1941. The nation had been gearing up for war even before the attack, and had been aiding its allies in Europe against the threat of Germany's Nazis under Adolf Hitler. When President Franklin D. Roosevelt announced U.S. entry into the war, it was on both the European and Pacific fronts, against both Japan and its allies and Germany and its allies.

U.S. armed forces were still rigidly segregated at the start of the war. So was the entertainment offered to the troops. The United Service Organizations (USO) existed to provide entertainment for military personnel at home and abroad, and there were black shows for black troops and white shows for white troops. One of the black shows was called *Tabloid Troupe Number 65*. The well-known white magician John Mulholland recommended Sanders, whom he had met at the *Magic on Broadway* show.

Sanders signed a contract to join the USO show, which was to tour black troop encampments in the American Southwest and West. One week before the show was to begin, Irene Sanders contracted pneumonia and died. Sanders availed himself of two weeks' "compassion leave" and then joined the show in Dallas, Texas. Arriving there, he was surprised to find that he was listed under "song and dance." He protested that he was a magician, not a song-and-dance man, but to no avail. Not knowing what to do with a black entertainer who neither sang, danced, nor played a musical instrument, the tour operators made him manager of the *Swing Time Revue*. Sanders was unhappy about not being able to use his talent as a magician, but he was a firm supporter of the war, and wanted to do whatever he could to make life more bearable for the segregated black troops. He was able to work his Punch and Judy puppet show routine into the show on occasion. The *Swing Time Revue* featured a young singer named Pearl Bailey in her second USO tour. Sanders and Bailey dated for a while. However, Bailey was determined to make it to stardom and said she had no time for a serious relationship. When the tour reached Los Angeles, she left to accept a booking at the city's famous Flamingo Club.

Sanders also left the *Swing Time Revue* in Los Angeles. He had been reassigned by the USO as manager of the *Suntan Revue* out of Atlanta, Georgia. This show entertained in hospitals where wounded black soldiers were also segregated from their white fellows. Sanders was able to include his magic act in this show, and he was delighted to perform his routines for convalescing black soldiers.

The *Suntan Revue* featured two sisters who were billed as acrobatic ballet specialists. The younger sister, eighteen-year-old Mildred Reed, looked incredibly like Sanders's late wife, Irene. After dating her for a time, Sanders married Mildred. The couple remained with the USO until 1945, when the war ended.

Sanders and his wife then went to New York, where he secured a booking performing close-up magic at the Harlem-on-the-Hudson Club. A tent card on each table announced Sanders's availability to perform a private magic show for patrons, and interested patrons would summon him to demonstrate his sleight-of-hand at the table. Sanders delighted his customers and often received big tips, which, added to his base salary of seventy-five dollars a week, represented a very comfortable living. However, he eventually returned to Washington, D.C., and to the black school circuit he most enjoyed.

A daughter, Carolyn, was born to Fetaque and Mildred Sanders in 1946, while the two were on the road in Pittsburgh, Pennsylvania. Sanders adapted a section of their trailer to make a nursery, and was quite content to travel with his family. His wife, however, thought differently. Concerned that their daughter be raised in a stable environment, Mildred Sanders left with four-year-old Carolyn and returned to Washington, D.C. The couple later divorced. Sanders once commented, "I wore out three trailers and two wives in my travels. Heaven took my first wife and the devil took the other."

A solo act again, Sanders continued on the black school circuit. He'd gotten some important media attention in the late 1940s, including an article in *Conjurers Magazine*, October 1946, and was featured in a December 1949 *Ebony* magazine article on black magicians. He used this material in his promotional pieces and secured more bookings, and for nearly a decade criss-crossed the country performing.

Being a solo, itinerant performer was difficult, and in 1958 Sanders suffered a stroke brought on by overwork. His peripheral vision was permanently impaired by the stroke, and in 1962 at the age of forty-seven he was forced to retire from active and regular performing. Although he still performed from time to time, he could no longer manage the kind of schedule he had kept up before his illness. He returned to Nashville and bought a house across the street from his parents. After his father died later that year, he moved in with his mother across the street.

Although he was semi-retired from magic, Sanders kept up with the latest tricks, corresponded with other magicians, and wrote frequently to magic magazines. He had kept his trailer and his own magic equipment, and he began to collect magic mate-

EBONY MAGICIANS

Fetaque Sanders is rated among best of present-day Negro magicians. Nashville-born trickster has been professional since 15, financed college education at Tennessee State by staging shows. He toured with USO during war.

EXPENSIVE PROPS and long hours of tedious practice are among chief reasons for so few Negroes pursuing careers in magic today. But limited outlet for talent has also been a discouraging factor as some booking agents claim there are few requests for Negro novelty acts unless they are disguised as some other race. Some have been able to overcome prejudice against Negro acts. Conjurors' Magazine publisher Edward W. Dart claims Negroes do not ha....... getting bookings if they are "clever" enough. ...... comment that "if I had the Privil............ to ex-Tennessee State College magicia.......... do so without hesitation .... Turk, or any oth.......

Fetaque Sanders bridged the era of discrimination and the era of equal rights for blacks. While most of his work was before black audiences, he occasionally performed with white shows. He influenced many younger people, who carry on his legacy in a much more welcoming racial atmosphere.

Courtesy of Dave Price

rials, concentrating especially on rare apparatus, books, posters, and photographs. Eventually, he had amassed enough to have his own private magic museum. He was responsive to inquiries from young aspiring magicians and in his later years became a sort of elder statesman of the magic world.

In March 1983, Sanders was out looking for magic material in second-hand stores when he was struck by a car. He never fully recovered and spent the last nine years of his life as an invalid. His mother had died in 1980, and afflicted with failing kidneys and requiring dialysis every two days, he was forced to sell the family home and move into the Carriage Health Care Center in Nashville. "I don't do tricks here," he told a reporter for the *Nashville Banner* in 1991. "People ask me, but I can't. Unless you're prepared, it can't be done the way it ought to. I'm smart enough to know that I'm not as smart as I think I am." He added, "The only thing I have to worry about now is having three hots [hot meals] a day and that's what I get here. . . . That's show business."

Fetaque Sanders died of complications from pneumonia on June 2, 1992. Many of the young magicians he inspired and helped became successful in the field. And they were luckier than he. They did not face the same racial barriers.

Chapter 9

Black Magicians in a Changing American Society

FRANK BRENTS

Among the young magicians Fetaque Sanders inspired was Frank Brents, the first African-American magician to appear on television. Brents was born in Louisville, Kentucky, in 1926. His first exposure to magic was seeing Fetaque Sanders perform at his school. Curious about how Sanders accomplished his illusions, young Brents bought a book about magic and practiced a few tricks. By 1937, at age eleven, he was performing in schools around Louisville. He continued his act for ten years, and in 1947 he was asked by a local television station to help in its promotion by doing his act at the studio. Brents seized the opportunity to advertise himself and had a series that ran for fifteen minutes each day.

Drafted into the army in 1950, Brents feared that his career as a magician might be interrupted. His superiors recognized his special gifts, however, and Brents was assigned to Special Services. Like the privately run United Service Organizations (USO), this division of the army provided entertainment for U.S. troops at home and abroad. While performing his magic act for American troops in Germany in 1951, Brents met his first fellow magician, a card-trick specialist named Paul LePaul.

When Brents joined the army, the U.S. military was finally beginning to integrate. World War II (1939–1945) had brought about many changes in American society and afforded a number of opportunities for blacks. Many were able to get jobs in the booming wartime industries. Some who joined the military had the chance to serve in combat roles. Black American units served with French units in Europe. Black pilots specially trained in a program at the black Tuskegee Institute in Alabama distinguished themselves in North Africa.

Blacks also benefited from the change in attitude that came over many white Americans because of the racial overtones in the war against Nazi Germany. The German Fuhrer Adolf Hitler was exterminating Jews, gypsies, and others because they were not of pure "Aryan" (by which he meant Caucasian) stock. Many Americans realized the irony of fighting abroad to "make the world safe for democracy" when they were guilty of discriminating against blacks in their own country. In 1948, after the war was over, President Harry S Truman outlawed discrimination in the armed forces. The military led the way in granting equal rights to blacks. Eventually, the rest of the nation followed.

On his discharge from the army in 1953, Brents moved to New York City, where he got a job working with the U.S. Postal

Service. Although he performed at nightclubs on weekends, he did not seriously consider making a full-time career of magic. After a while he found he was getting so many bookings that he didn't have time for his post office job. He was especially popular at Latino vaudeville clubs, and since New York's Latino population had burgeoned after World War II, he was rarely without work. During the summer, he performed at the major resorts in the Catskill Mountains. He had the distinction of performing at two lawn parties given by the Kennedy family when John F. Kennedy was president of the United States (1961–1963).

Having gotten a taste of international travel while he was in the army, Brents was eager to go back abroad to perform. In 1965, he signed on with the Albert Travel Agency in Paris, France, the major entertainment booking agency in Europe at that time. He already did his act to music, and he found that music and magic were understood in any culture. For the next fifteen years, he toured regularly in Europe, Asia, Latin America, and Africa. Not only did he perform on foreign stages, he also made many international television appearances, including the *David Nixon Show* in London, England and *El Show de Rene* in Caracas, Venezuela, as well as shows in France, Germany, Italy, Spain, and Japan.

When he was stateside, he continued to be one of the few black magicians on American television. He made six appearances on *Bozo the Clown* and fifteen on *Captain Kangaroo*. Although most of his American television work was on children's shows, he also appeared on *The Jerry Lewis Show*.

Like many other magicians, Brents did a dove act. But one of his best-known tricks was the "Duck Act." He would shake a silk scarf and a duck would fall out. He would shake the scarf again and produce another duck. After a show, he would bring a trained duck out to visit with the audience. In 1970, at the International Brotherhood of Magicians/Society of American Magicians combined annual magic show in New York, Brents did a version of his "Duck Act," producing a huge duck as his finale.

Besides what he calls "duck magic," Brents specializes in comedy magic, close-up magic, and mentalism. For many years, Brents performed mostly abroad, where he found he could make more money than in his native country. His publicity material asserts that he has spun his magic spells in more than forty countries, including appearances at "the Olympia Theater in Paris, the Friedrichstadtpalast in Berlin, the Loew's Hotel in Monte Carlo, London's Churchill Club, plus theaters and nightclubs in such exotic locations as Bali, Tahiti, Peru, Kenya, Hong Kong, Japan, and South Africa. He has performed for King Juan Carlos of Spain, Princess Grace of Monaco, and the Rockefellers and Kennedys. Additionally, he has shared the bill with superstars such as Shirley Jones, Rita Moreno, Red Buttons, Dom Deluise, Flip Wilson, Vic Damone, Sidney Poitier, Danny Kaye, Isabelle Sanford, Buddy Hackett, and Ed Sullivan." Often, he even performed magic while getting from one place to another, doing mentalist routines as well as his illusions on cruise ships.

Because of his bookings abroad and his work on cruise ships, Brents continues to be on the road as much as ten months out of the year. When he is home in New York, he often appears at the Monday Night Magic shows at the Sullivan Street Playhouse in Greenwich Village, where he performs close-up magic

Frank Brents & his TECHNICOLOR DOVES

Frank Brents, shown here with the magician's traditional
doves, was the first black magician to appear on television,
in 1947. He spent much of his early career performing
abroad, but in recent years has gotten many bookings
in the United States.

in the Gallery. In the summertime, he performs at resorts in the Catskill Mountains. Like Fetaque Sanders, the man who inspired him to become a magician, Frank Brents has managed to make his passion his career.

ODIS PRICE

Unlike Frank Brents, Odis Price was not able to make a career as a magician. But he sought out young blacks to teach and encouraged them to dream of doing what he did not. When he was young, he'd been privileged to see a black magician. He wanted other kids to have that same opportunity. As he said to Barry Glassner, who wrote an extensive article on black magicians for the January 1977 issue of *Sepia* magazine, "In the past there were not many blacks performing magic simply because we didn't have any black magicians. And black kids didn't have the slightest idea of how someone goes about becoming a magician."

Price was an exception. When he was twelve, a black magician appeared at his school in North Carolina, and he was so fascinated by the performance that he determined to find out how to do magic himself. He eventually located an amateur magician in a neighboring town, who gave him the address of a magic shop with a mail-order catalogue. The first trick Price ordered cost fifty cents and involved twirling a handkerchief and producing a ring. From then on, whenever Price saved enough money, he ordered more tricks.

Price entertained his friends with magic while in high school. After serving in the army, he settled in Woodbridge, Virginia, not far from Washington, D.C., and picked up magic

A New Take on
the Underwater Escape

In the late 1950s, a black Chicagoan named Jack Hall attempted to follow in the footsteps of the great Harry Houdini. A postal employee and expert swimmer, Hall called himself the world's greatest escape artist. He pointed out that Houdini, when he was bound with ropes and submerged underwater, would emerge untied in thirty seconds. Hall, by contrast, could remain underwater for up to an hour.

Hall's version of the underwater escape was to be swathed in 126 feet of cloth like an Egyptian mummy and then bound securely from head to toe with two ropes, which were tied in eight knots. He would then somersault into the water, swim one-eighth of a mile, and free himself. He had also perfected four different variations on his act. Although Hall planned to do the trick professionally, he was unsuccessful in making a career as an escape artist. Harry Houdini's fame remained unassailed.

again. Around 1972, a woman in his neighborhood asked him to perform at a children's party. Price pretended that he had a full performing schedule but would try to squeeze the children's party in. He had no idea what to charge, and asked for ten dollars.

"That first show was one of the most terrifying experiences of my life," Price told Barry Glassner of *Sepia* in 1977. "The kids kept screaming out that they knew how I did the tricks, and sometimes they were even correct in their guesses. I was so frustrated by the end of the show that I swore I would never perform again. But later a kindergarten asked me to do a show and wouldn't accept 'no' for an answer. That time the kids loved me, and I've been performing ever since."

Price was unable to make a living at magic and held a regular job at Safeway Supermarket. Still, he was glad to have the money he earned performing—twenty-five dollars for children's shows and sixty dollars for stage shows for adults—to augment his income. But making money was not his main objective. He believed that magic was a great motivator for young people and good preparation for other careers. He even designed a course in magic for children.

"A problem I have found is that nearly all of the children who enroll for my magic courses are whites," Price told Glassner. "Black kids just do not find out about these things from their parents or friends, and when they do find out, they cannot afford the equipment or the lessons." The few African-American children who did come to him for lessons were, he believed, more likely to succeed than the whites. "Young black magicians actually have an advantage sometimes over new white magicians," he observed. "There are still not many of us, so we get instant attention. In show business, the more unique you are the better off you are."

While blacks in all fields still struggled for equal opportunity in the 1950s, the generation that came of age during and after the 1960s had a world of possibilities open to them. The civil rights movement of the 1960s brought about a major transformation in race relations in the United States. It led to improved conditions for blacks in all areas of activity. No longer was racial discrimination and segregation the law of the land. In fact, racial inclusion was. Although discrimination still existed, blacks had real opportunities in many fields. For black magicians, as Odis Price pointed out, being black was an edge, because they were unique.

GOLDFINGER AND DOVE

Just two years before Price made that statement, a black magician with a unique act was finally making it big. As Goldfinger and Dove, Jack Vaughn and his wife/assistant infused magic with a glamour that no black magician had ever achieved before.

Goldfinger was born Jack Vaughn in Cleveland, Ohio, in 1948. He became interested in magic after he started watching a television show called *The Magic Land of Alakazam*, starring magician Mark Wilson. Vaughn was soon buying inexpensive magic kits and dreaming of becoming successful. His family and friends warned him that magic was "a white man's profession," but he persevered. "I'm happy to say they were wrong," he told a reporter for *Ebony* in 1977. "I didn't find a color barrier in professional magic; what I found was a talent barrier. You can't get anywhere fast in magic if your act isn't smooth and practiced. But when you're good, you're good, and no one cares what color you are."

As a child, Vaughn taught himself as much magic as he could. Soon, he was looking for someone to teach him more complicated tricks. In 1956, he happened to attend a Halloween fair at a local Catholic church, at which the parish priest, an amateur magician, performed a magic show. Eager to learn the priest's tricks, Vaughn agreed to attend the church if the priest would teach him a new trick each Sunday. By the age of eight, he was able to frighten away a bully who was threatening him by making a rock disappear and promising to do the same thing to the bully.

Young Jack Vaughn proved particularly adept at sleight-of-hand tricks. It is said that a local mystic predicted that his "golden fingers" would bring him fame and fortune. After that, people began to call him Goldfinger.

Vaughn soon exhausted the priest's repertoire and had to seek out professional magicians in the city to teach him. In 1963, when he was fifteen, he saw a newspaper advertisement for magic lessons and became a pupil of Clarence "Chandu" Hunter. Hunter not only schooled the young Vaughn in the tricks of the trade but eventually allowed him to open for Hunter's own act. He also arranged for Vaughn's first publicity photos. When Jack Vaughn was ready to perform on his own, Hunter booked his first performances and chauffeured him to and from them.

By the time he entered college, Vaughn had adopted the stage name Goldfinger and was performing regularly in and around Cleveland. He was in such demand that he soon left college to devote himself to performing full time.

When young American men started being drafted into the military to fight in Vietnam, Vaughn enlisted in the army. His talent for magic was soon discovered by his superiors. He was assigned to make friends among the inhabitants of Vietnamese jungle villages by doing magic tricks for them. The army made sure that he had all the props and animals he needed for his tricks. When he pulled rabbits or birds out of his top hat, he would give them away to the starving villagers, so they would have something to eat. He even performed on a television program in Saigon, the capital of South Vietnam.

While on leave in Hawaii in 1969, Vaughn visited a nightclub and met a native-born exotic dancer named Dove. They were soon married, beginning a lasting domestic and professional partnership. After Vaughn was honorably discharged from the army, he returned to the United States with his bride. The couple stayed in Cleveland only long enough for Dove to meet Vaughn's family and to have Hunter arrange for publicity photographs of them together. Then they set off for the West Coast to seek their fortune.

Together, the couple worked on and perfected what is called a "class act" in the profession. They dressed in formal evening clothes. Goldfinger, who was tall and thin, always dressed in a suit and hat. Dove wore beautiful gowns. She was an expert seamstress, and saved money by making their stage costumes. The couple featured perfectly choreographed dance numbers and crowd-pleasing tricks. Performing for twenty-five dollars a night at small black clubs in and around Los Angeles, Vaughn met a number of other young black magicians. He traded tricks and news of the magic profession with them. This small magic fraternity often met in Vaughn and his wife's Los Angeles apartment, where there was plenty of inspiration. Their apartment was crowded with stage costumes and magic paraphernalia. Part of one room was devoted to a large plastic pyramid that was not a show prop. Rather, it was the place where Vaughn sat and

As Goldfinger and Dove, Jack Vaughn and his wife/assistant infused magic with a glamour that no black magician had ever achieved before.

Courtesy of Jim Magus

East Meets West

One of Goldfinger and Dove's most popular routines was a pantomime skit entitled "East Meets West." The Asian Dove represented East, and the American Goldfinger was West. Goldfinger, dressed in a suit, top hat, and sunglasses, and carrying a cane, played the part of a man trying to woo a beautiful woman holding a flower, played by Dove. In an attempt to impress her, he caused the cane to float, spin, and dance, and finally to change into silk scarves. As he looked at her proudly, expecting the lady to be impressed, she handed him the flower. Suddenly, the cane appeared in her hands and began to dance. The flower in Goldfinger's hands wilted, representing his deflated ego.

meditated regularly. He was a member of a worldwide "pyramid power" group that believed that placing oneself inside pyramid-shaped devices increased one's personal energy. Out on the apartment's balcony were bird cages filled with doves they used in their performances.

A classic magic illusion is the "Broomstick Suspension," which is just what the title suggests: A magician causes a broomstick to be suspended in mid-air. Vaughn created a variation on this trick. Instead of a broomstick, Vaughn suspended Dove—horizontally across the point of a spear. According to

Jim Magus, author of *Magical Heroes: The Lives and Legends of Great African American Magicians*, Goldfinger and Dove were the first magicians to present the "Deluxe Card Castle," an illusion in which Goldfinger produced a house of cards from which Dove emerged.

Among the most dramatic routines Vaughn developed was an exhibition of fire-eating, a trick that had been taught him by Chandu Hunter. Not many magicians were willing to attempt that trick, but Vaughn did it successfully as part of his regular act.

Although the couple had a busy performance schedule, Vaughn continued to network with other local magicians and to visit the Magic Castle, the headquarters of a club for magicians in Hollywood, as often as he could. One night he saw the white magician Channing Pollock performing, and after the show he shyly approached the famous conjurer. Pollock mistook Vaughn for the club's parking valet and requested his car, only to learn that he had inadvertently insulted an up-and-coming young black magician. Pollock was embarrassed about his insensitivity. The following day he visited Vaughn, who was working at the Magic Mountain Amusement Park, and apologized for his error. The two became friends, and Pollock shared many of his performing tips with the younger magician.

In 1975 Goldfinger and Dove finally got their big break. For Jack Vaughn, it was "overnight success" after more than ten years of hard work. The couple were performing at a small black nightclub in Los Angeles one night when the comedian Redd Foxx was in the audience. Foxx, who in his early days had done stage magic, recognized their talent. He sought them out after the show and asked them to perform the opening act for his *Redd Foxx Show* at the Hacienda in Las Vegas, Nevada. All they needed was that one break. The same year, the couple were voted the Most Promising New Act in Hollywood. They appeared on several television shows, including *Sammy and Company*, Sammy Davis, Jr.'s show from Las Vegas. Davis, Jr. said the husband-and-wife team had "flash, originality and astonishing showmanship."

In 1977, the Magic Castle, the professional magicians' club in Los Angeles, California, estimated that there were two hundred professional magicians working in the United States. Of them, they named twenty-eight-year-old Jack Vaughn as one of the brightest newcomers to the profession. Goldfinger and Dove appeared on the Dinah Shore and Johnny Carson television shows and were regularly featured in comedian Redd Foxx's Las Vegas revue, at magic conventions, and on nightclub stages across the nation and abroad. In 1979, and again in 1983, they were named Stage Magicians of the Year by the Academy of Magical Arts in Los Angeles.

One of the keys to the success of Goldfinger and Dove was their continued effort to add new material to their routines. Early on, Vaughn had learned the "Three Card Monte" trick long used by close-up magicians. For it to work on stage and conform to his brand of special effects and larger-than-life magic, he used jumbo cards. According to Jim Magus, he was the first magician to present the routine entirely in pantomime. He played the roles of both the "Three Card Monte" hustler and the tricked passerby. His and Dove's best-known performance of the trick was not in pantomime but included audience participation on the nationally televised "World's Greatest Magic, Part 5."

The couple produced three jumbo cards, two Kings and a Queen, and showed both sides. They turned the Queen card

Ultimate Sword through Neck

"Show a large sword. The sword is nearly three feet long, is really sharp and is not a toy. You can show the sword to be absolutely solid. Thrust it through a head of cabbage. Bang it on the stage. Solid. Next, place a massive metal collar around the neck of an assistant from the audience! Instantly push the solid sword right through the neck of your assistant! The audience can see the sword penetrating the victim's neck! In one side and out the other! What an effect! Naturally, the girl is unharmed at the end of the effect! The sword is of Italian design, hand made by European craftsmen. We shipped one to Goldfinger and Dove in Puerto Rico. Goldfinger called us to tell us that he was absolutely thrilled with the props and would immediately add the routine to his act!

From Hank Lee's Magic Factory on-line catalogue, magicfact.com

around so that its back was to the audience. They turned the two Kings around as well. Vaughn then asked the audience to bet on which card was the Queen. Each time someone bet that a particular card was the Queen, it turned out to be a King. Again and again, the Queen would vanish from its spot and reappear elsewhere. The Queen card was never found by the audience, no matter how closely they watched.

In the summer of 1990, the Magic Castle in Los Angeles was featured for the first time in a television special. Goldfinger and Dove were the only illusionists of color among the nine acts in "The Magic of the Magic Castle" presented on CBS-TV. They were also the most glamorous.

Goldfinger and Dove continue to perform at home and abroad. The couple's special brand of showmanship and glamour keeps them popular decade after decade. Victor and Diamond, a younger couple who do glamorous stage magic, have modeled their act after that of Goldfinger and Dove and have also been successful, both in the United States and abroad.

10

Today's Black Magicians

Today, African-American magicians can be
found doing every type of magic—from glamorous stage acts like that of Goldfinger and
Dove and Victor and Diamond to close-up magic in restaurants.
They perform wherever magic is featured—in variety shows and
on television specials, in children's hospitals and at business
trade shows, not to mention church affairs and college campus-
es, the more traditional performing venues for black magicians.
There is no area of magic that a black magician cannot conquer,
and there is not room in this book to feature all the modern
black magicians. The following magicians represent the great
variety of work possible today.

LEMONT HASKINS

Lemont Haskins, whose specialty is close-up magic, might be called a "generalist." He has performed various types of magic, in a host of different settings. Haskins was born and raised in Harlem in New York City. He does not like to give out his birth date, saying, "I have been lying about my birth year for years. I don't want to get caught in the lie I have been telling by telling another lie." He was four years old when he saw his first magician—at Macy's department store downtown. "He was doing incredible things with these coins," says Haskins, "making them go in and out of his head, through his foot. . . . I stood there in total amazement. My mother was calling me and I didn't hear. I was scolded for that."

From then on, Haskins was hooked on magic. He went to magic shows and watched them on television and became quite good at figuring out how the tricks were done. When he was twelve years old, his uncle took him to a company Christmas party at which a magician performed. Haskins recalls, "Presto came out, and for the first time I saw a magician who looked like me."

Presto, born Everett Earl Johnson in 1931, used that stage name when he did children's shows. He was once credited by *Magic* magazine with introducing more young black men to the magic fraternity than any individual alive. Lemont Haskins was one of them. Rather than being awed by Presto, Haskins decided to show off by revealing the secrets of Presto's tricks to his fellow audience members. "Presto saw that I was a troublemaker, breaking his rhythm," says Haskins. "True professional that he was, he decided that the best thing to do was bring me up on stage with him as an assistant. He gave me a magic wand that would bend every time I held it, but I figured out how to make it stay straight. He tried several things like that, but I was too smart for him. So eventually he got rid of me by asking me to take some of his magic things back into his dressing room for him. I had a great time going through his stuff and seeing how things worked.

"When he came back to the dressing room after the show, I begged him to tell me how I could learn all those tricks. He wrote down the address of Tannen's Magic Shop for me. From then on, I spent my Saturdays at Tannen's, watching the professionals doing tricks for each other and taking some lessons from one of the resident pros."

One Saturday, after leaving Tannen's on West 25TH Street in the Chelsea section of Manhattan, Haskins saw a street magician performing. It was not unusual to see street magicians, but this man was black. "I was amazed to see people giving him money after his show," says Haskins, who introduced himself and was surprised that the street magician encouraged him to do a show of his own right there. "People gave me seven dollars, and I was hooked. I started performing on the streets, and soon I was making more money doing street magic on weekends than my mother made at her job the entire week. I was on my way."

Haskins did not consider street magic a proper career, so he joined local theater groups to perfect his performing skills. Among the groups he performed with was the Salt and Pepper Mime Theater. For further training in the art of illusion, he attended Tannen's Magic Camp, where he won prizes, including

Lemont Haskins is a generalist who has performed many
types of magic in different venues, including the Clown
Care Unit of the Big Apple Circus.

Courtesy of Lemont Haskins

first place in advanced stage presentation. He also studied privately with several white magicians.

Haskins, who goes by the stage name Magic Monty, has had a varied career. For a time, he worked at the Apollo Theatre in Harlem. Probably the most famous theater where blacks performed from the 1930s to the 1960s, the Apollo was renowned for its amateur nights that gave breaks to some of the best black entertainers. Unsuccessful acts were dragged from the stage with a large, hooked cane. Closed for two decades, the Apollo reopened in the 1980s. Haskins worked an extended engagement at the revived amateur nights as the "take-off man." He used physical comedy and improvisation to remove undesirable acts from the stage and earned the nickname "The Executioner."

For several years, Haskins was a member of the Clown Care Unit (CCU) of the Big Apple Circus. Founded in 1977 as a not-for-profit performing arts organization, the Big Apple Circus is dedicated to presenting the finest classical circus in America. They also engage in a number of outreach efforts, including the Clown Care Unit, a program in which performers dress up as clowns and tour local hospitals, entertaining sick children. Haskins, who first worked in the Big Apple Circus as a tent magician, found that working with sick children was more to his liking. As one of the CCU's regular "doctors of delight" at Harlem Hospital, he made "clown rounds," a parody of medical rounds, where the healing power of humor is the chief medical treatment. In 1994, the Clown Care Unit won a Wallenburg Humanitarian Award for its work with sick children.

As a stage magician, Haskins has toured in eight countries, including Japan and Egypt. He has appeared on television in the United States and abroad. He has done street magic at

South Street Seaport in New York City and appeared in a commercial for Daffy's clothing store as a street hustler tricking innocent passersby with "Three Card Monte." He has also appeared in commercials for Burger King, NYNEX, Bell Atlantic, and the Connecticut Lottery. He has done promotional work for Seagram and Canon and worked trade shows for J. Walter Thompson, among other companies. Recently, he has performed at Catskill Mountains resorts. In the variety of magic he can do, and the range of venues he is comfortable performing in, Haskins carries on the tradition of the itinerant magician.

CHARLES GREENE III

While Lemont Haskins does occasional business trade shows, Charles Greene III has made a specialty of them. He has further specialized by using magic tricks—he always calls them illusions—to promote highly technical products. Often, this requires learning a considerable amount of information about the products so he can create an illusion that fits. As an example, when asked to demonstrate the effectiveness of cleaning agents in such detergents as Tide and Cheer, he made soiled handkerchiefs magically become clean while discussing the merits of the chemicals.

Born in Houston, Texas, in 1961, Greene, who was named after both his father and his grandfather, grew up in Hackensack, New Jersey, where he attended the Hackensack Christian School. He became interested in science at an early age and was the proud owner of a chemistry set before the age of ten. With it, he investigated the properties of various materials. He didn't know that he would later be able to apply what he had learned to the field of magic.

Greene recalls seeing a magician perform at his neighborhood church once. However, his fascination with magic did not begin there. When he was ten years old, he received a magic catalog as a gift. The tricks arrayed on its pages opened up the world of magic for him. He ordered items that interested him and studied the secrets behind common magic tricks. Soon, he was in demand to perform at private parties. Greene's parents encouraged him and saw to it that he met the best magicians in the area.

From about ages fifteen to twenty, Greene traveled by bus to New York City each Saturday morning to visit Tannen's Magic Shop. There, he pored over books and traded magic tricks with other magicians. After several hours at Tannen's, he would go to Governor's Restaurant, which no longer exists but was a popular hangout for magicians. At the shop and the restaurant, he met magicians both amateur and professional, unknown and well known. The late Doug Henning, already famous, became one of his tutors.

Greene had just graduated from high school when he was offered a job as a magician at a Six Flags Great Adventure production company in Jackson, New Jersey. After a year with that company, he transferred to Six Flags Astro World in Houston, Texas. In Houston, Greene met a fellow magician named John Carney, who specialized in magic acts at restaurants. By the early 1980s, magic-themed restaurants were becoming popular. Diners at these restaurants were treated to special entertainment as magicians went from table to table doing tricks. At some restaurants, there were also special floor shows. Greene recog-

CHARLES GREENE III

CORPORATE MAGICIAN

Featured in *The Wall Street Journal, Discover* and *Successful Meetings.*

Charles Greene III has made a specialty of technical
trade-show magic, one of the few magicians today with
this unique specialty.

Courtesy of Charles Greene

nized he had another forum for his illusions. When the Six Flags troupe relocated to California the following year, Greene stayed in Houston. Entertaining clients as they waited to be seated, or going from table to table performing for seated diners, Greene soon had more work than he could handle. At one point, he was performing at nine different restaurants and hotels in the city. Paid an agreed-upon sum by each hotel and restaurant, Greene refused tips from patrons, feeling that to accept them was beneath his dignity. This policy of Greene's did not endear him to other restaurant magicians, who happily accepted all tips.

Nevertheless, they did not allow their resentment to diminish their respect for his skill as a magician. For two years in a row, Greene's fellow magicians voted him Houston's Best Close-Up Entertainer. In 1982, the year he won his second such award, Greene performed at the Las Vegas Desert Magic Seminar and won the Silver Lion Award for his performance of close-up coin magic. In September of that year, he secured his first week-long booking at the Magic Castle in Los Angeles, California, the best-known magic establishment in the nation.

His restaurant work brought Charles Greene to the world of the business trade show. Diners who also happened to be businessmen realized that Greene's illusions would be entertaining for their trade-show clients. The first company he worked for was Pyramid of Houston, which employed him to promote their quick-drying cement. Soon, he was working with the marketing and sales directors for other major companies to create magic acts for trade shows, and receiving $1,500 a day, plus expenses, for his trouble.

Magic acts have been standard fare at trade shows for years, but very rarely has the magician been black. Clarence "Chandu" Hunter did occasional trade shows. *The Success Book*, published in 1973 by Magic, Inc., contains a picture of a Chicago magician named Sammy Martin, identified as "probably the first black magician to appear at a trade show," and added that he was working at making the form a career. Though Lemont Haskins does occasional trade shows, Charles Greene is unique in concentrating exclusively on trade-show magic and in specializing in technical industries.

At first, Greene merely took his standard illusions to the trade-show floor. One of the most popular was a "mind-reading" illusion he had first developed in his days puttering around with his chemistry set. He would ask a member of the audience to write something on an index card with a magic marker. He would then ask the audience member to seal the card in a white envelope. Taking the envelope, Greene would pour lighter fluid over it and set it afire. Then he would "read the ashes" to discover what had been written on the card. The trick was very simple: Any standard white envelope becomes transparent once lighter fluid is poured over it. In the course of dowsing the envelope with fluid, Greene would read the words on the card inside.

It was not long before Greene realized he would get more business if he could adapt his standard tricks—or create new ones—that had some reference to the product he was supposed to promote. So, when asked to promote an oil-filtration medium composed mostly of walnut shells, he decided to include in his act the time-tested shell game, which featured three walnut shells.

Greene used the rope illusion—in which he revealed that three apparently equal lengths of rope were actually three different lengths—to demonstrate the point that several products can be related without being identical. He suspended an audi-

Corporate Card Tricks

Charles Greene III found that adaptations of card tricks were especially popular. In one, a card with the company's name written on it always mysteriously comes out on top, as proof that the company is "ahead of the pack."

He developed another card trick for Conoco Products when that company asked him to promote its new flow improver at an American Petroleum Institute Pipeline Conference. Greene puzzled over how to feature the substance, which reduces drag in oil pipelines. Finally, he came up with a card trick. Taking a deck of cards, he wrote words describing some of the properties of Flow Improver on the side of the deck. He then worked out a way to shuffle the deck of cards and still have the words show up. As an example, he would write "Reduces drag" on the side of the deck. Ordinarily, shuffling the deck would break up the letters so the words are not readable. Magically Charles Greene's deck of cards would always end up with "Reduces drag" written on the side. He has never revealed how he does it. The trick, which he also uses when representing pharmaceutical companies, is always a great success.

In 1988, when Greene decided to establish his own company, he named his enterprise Corporate Shuffle.

ence member in mid-air to show that the company he was representing offered support "wherever you go."

As a corporate-trade-show magician, Charles Greene had to be more than just an entertainer. He also had to be a teacher, but in a highly entertaining way. He was so good at his chosen specialty that he was soon getting more business than he could handle alone. He had to hire an office manager and a writer to help him prepare scripted shows.

To keep his hand in the world of magic where he got his start, Greene spends two weeks each year performing in a Houston nightclub, trying out new illusions. He also practices an hour or two every day. Not well known in the world of nightclub entertainment, Charles Greene nevertheless has carved out a lucrative niche for himself. He understands that he can, in a unique way, create a positive feeling associated with the products he represents. This has been good for the companies that hire him and good for his business.

In the 1990s, Greene moved from Houston to Washington, D.C., a more centralized place from which to travel. His specialty involves a lot of touring, not only in the United States but also abroad. He has performed at health-care trade shows in Canada, Germany, Mexico, Sweden, Monaco, and even Egypt.

The busiest times of the year for Greene are fall and spring, when most trade shows are held. In the slow months, he performs at local clubs around Washington, D.C., and practicing at home. He attends local magic conferences and at one saw a young amateur magician, who goes by the stage name Rahaan, perform. After seeing Rahaan perform at another conference, he called him. He then served as mentor to the young man, teaching him not only tricks but how to market himself.

Greene's advice to young magicians is to stay in school and get as much formal education as they possibly can. He explains, "it may seem as if to be a good magician all you have to do is great magic. That is not true. Having a successful career in magic will require that you have knowledge in many different areas, including negotiating, speaking, marketing, travel, hospitality, etc. As magic should be, it looks easy. However, hard work and persistence in pursuing goals will pay off. Today, I read more books on business, marketing, and finance than I do on magic. The magic is important, but much more is required."

DAVID BLAINE

While Charles Greene, dressed in a three-piece suit, plies his magic at corporate trade shows, David Blaine does street magic wearing jeans and a T-shirt. It is one of the ironies of current popular culture that a street magician should be the star of not one but three television specials in less than five years. Blaine is the first magician of color to have his own magic special on television. The broadcast on ABC-TV of "David Blaine: Street Magic" in May 1997 established Blaine as magic's newest star. It also created an uproar among United States magicians who had refused to take him seriously. This "hip hop Houdini" may have single-handedly ushered in a new era of magic.

Blaine is deliberately mysterious about his background. When asked about his early life by Joyce Wadler of the *New York Times* in December 2000, he gave some precise information, but suggested ". . . we should give it some twists. You should never be accurate. You should be entertaining. Houdini,

Chaplin [the great actor Charlie Chaplin], they always told conflicting stories." He told Wadler that his mother was of Russian Jewish heritage. But according to another source, his mother's name was Patrice White, which is hardly a Russian Jewish name. Blaine told Wadler that his father was of Puerto Rican and Italian descent. If that is correct, then his father must have been of black Puerto Rican heritage. Blaine is actually David's middle name. He has never revealed his real last name. Over the years he has used several surnames, including those of his grandfather and stepfather. It is probably not just a desire to be mysterious that drives David Blaine to be obscure about his personal life; it is a fierce protectiveness as well.

According to Blaine, his father was a Vietnam veteran. He was also an alcoholic and a drug addict who left the family for good in 1976, when David was three. His mother, a teacher and waitress, worked three jobs to support herself and her son and to send David to good schools.

When David was four, she bought him a trick that allowed him to pass a pencil through a playing card. He was soon climbing up on tables and performing for any adult who would pay attention. His mother encouraged him to develop his skill and, according to Blaine, made him want to be the best he could be.

When Blaine was eleven, he moved with his mother to Passaic, New Jersey. By that time, he had started creating games of physical challenge to test himself. In Passaic, he began practicing levitation, the illusion of magically lifting himself off the ground. He amazed his mother, his friends, and everyone else for whom he performed the trick.

Blaine was attending Passaic High School when his mother became ill with ovarian cancer. He did all he could to care for her. When she decided to try a macrobiotic diet, he got a job in a macrobiotic restaurant so he could give her meals for free. Sadly, no diet or medical treatment worked. After his mother died in 1994, the twenty-one-year-old Blaine moved to Manhattan, where he slept on friends' couches and took acting classes at the Neighborhood Playhouse. He began performing on the street, a form of entertainment with a long tradition in American cities. In the poor neighborhoods where he lived, he would set up a folding table and, with a deck of cards, do tricks for passersby. He used no props or costumes. It was just David Blaine and his deck of cards entertaining people on the street for tips. From time to time, he would vary his routine, guessing how much change people had in their pockets, or telling them what card they were thinking of.

Although he was most comfortable on the streets, Blaine realized he would have to make connections with influential people if he wanted to be a success. He began frequenting downtown clubs. Whenever he recognized a celebrity, he would walk up and introduce himself. Spotting Al Pacino one evening, he went over to introduce himself and do a card trick. Pacino brushed him off. Undaunted, Blaine returned a few minutes later to try again. Taking a deck of cards from his jeans pocket, he said to Pacino, "pick a card," and soon he had the actor counting out ten more cards and then sitting on all eleven. When the chosen card somehow "jumped" back to the deck, Pacino was flabbergasted. He later became a friend of Blaine's.

In the same way, Blaine got to know actors Robert De Niro and Arnold Schwarzenneger, singer Madonna, boxer Mike Tyson, and other celebrities. Soon he was performing at celebrity parties, earning three to five hundred dollars an hour, and

David Blaine has been successful in bringing "street magic" to television. He is the only magician of color to have had three television specials.

AP Photo by Donna Svennevik, Courtesy of ABC-TV

also performing at trendy downtown hangouts like the Bowery Bar and Cafe Tabac. The director Woody Allen invited him to perform tricks for the cast and crew of his film *Everyone Says I Love You*. Spike Lee, whom Blaine met at the premiere of the filmmaker's movie, *Clockers*, was so impressed with Blaine's talent that he agreed to shoot the promotional piece for Blaine's first TV special.

Blaine managed to get the special through Jon Podell, a music agent with International Creative Management. When Podell voiced doubts that Blaine's low-key, close-up magic would work on television, Blaine hired a video crew and produced a ten-minute demo tape to convince him. Persuaded, Podell took the tape to ABC Entertainment, whose president at the time, Jamie Tarses, later told *Time* magazine, "It's a roll of the dice. But David is very contemporary, of his generation, hip, cool. We think he can pull in the young, urban audience."

The special, which ran during the annual May "sweeps week," was well received and got high ratings. Mostly featuring an endless number of card tricks performed in various cities, it became as riveting to television viewers as to the street audience when Blaine levitated at least four inches off the ground. Two months later, on a segment of *Oprah*, called "Summer Magic," he performed his levitation again. As private about his tricks as about his real last name, Blaine refused to reveal his secret. Magic aficionados knew that it was a variation on the "Balducci Levitation."

That Blaine, a relative newcomer, managed to get a TV special did not sit well with many other magicians. They charged that Blaine did not do any original tricks. Responding to that criticism, the producer of the special countered that if other magicians were more deserving, perhaps they should get better agents.

Blaine had his own way of responding to that criticism. Long having tested himself with physical challenges, he decided to make such a challenge the basis of his next TV special. A great fan of Harry Houdini, he chose to perform a trick that Houdini had never accomplished but had always wanted to do. He would be "buried alive" for a week. But Blaine elected to spend seven days submerged in a Plexiglass box inside a water-filled Plexiglass tank in a hole dug into the ground in front of millionaire Donald Trump's new high-rise development on the shores of the Hudson River.

Actually, there was no trickery about it. Staying in that box for seven days was a test of endurance. Blaine prepared for the feat by fasting for some time. This would allow him to sur-

The Balducci Levitation

David Blaine's television special was barely over when magicians and fans of magic were on the Internet trying to figure out how he levitated. Soon, an explanation of the trick was available to all. In fact, the secrets to many magic tricks are available on the Worldwide Web. Even if the explanations to be found there are accurate, not everyone can *do* the trick.

The "Balducci Levitation" is very difficult. It all depends on angles. You must stand at a 45 degree angle about ten feet away from the audience, so they can only see one of your feet. You stand on tiptoe with the foot the audience cannot see. Without attesting to its accuracy, and with a warning that the following explanation of a very difficult illusion seems very simplified, here is how the secret is described on one web site:

"All you do is pretend to 'float' off of the ground while you tippee-toe on just one foot (the foot furthest from their view). . . . Believe it or not, this looks GREAT! The small audience cannot see your supporting foot because it is hidden by three things: your pants, the angle of the trick, and your closest shoe (which hides their view of the foot being used to 'levitate' you.) You might only rise three or five inches off of the ground, but it's all in the presentation! You will want to slowly rise off the ground . . . wait just one second, and then drop fast. Stay up too long and they will probably figure it out."

vive without food and would diminish the amount of body waste he would eliminate.

On the appointed day, he stepped into the plastic box wearing pajamas. He had a blanket with him, and a stuffed animal. The box was equipped with an apparatus that delivered a minimal amount of oxygen. Lowered to a depth of about six feet in a tank containing 4,000 pounds of water, Blaine settled down for an ordeal of seven days and seven nights when he would have a mere four tablespoons of water for nourishment.

Perhaps a far greater ordeal than having to go without food for seven days was Blaine's choice to stay in a transparent underwater "coffin," visible from ground level. For the next week, thousands upon thousands of fans and curiosity seekers filed by the spot, often standing in line for two hours or more to get a look at Blaine. When he was not sleeping, he acknowledged his audience with a smile or a wave, which grew weaker as time went on.

Blaine's burial stunt was the talk of New York that week. Regis Philbin, Barbara Walters, Rosie O'Donnell, and a niece of Harry Houdini visited him there. When the seven days were over, a very weak David Blaine emerged from his Plexiglass coffin. Among the first things he did was to take a long hot bubble bath, during which he started thinking about his next publicity stunt.

That next stunt was for Blaine to be frozen alive. For his third ABC-TV special, which aired in late November 2000, Blaine was buried in an ice "coffin" for sixty-two hours. The one-hour special included taped footage of his burial and of occasional checking-in on his progress, complete with shots of the crowds that gathered to watch him and the celebrity friends

Unseasonably warm weather complicated David Blaine's
"ice coffin" stunt in November 2000. There was a chance
that the ice block would collapse.

Photograph courtesy of Timothy Travaglini

who came by to cheer him on. Interspersed with these segments were taped footage of him pursuing his first and greatest love, street magic: just being out on the streets of a city, doing illusions, and interacting with passersby. His disinterment from the ice block was broadcast live.

To prepare for this stunt, Blaine spent months immersing himself in ice baths. He also trained himself to sleep standing up. Meanwhile, he ordered a six-ton block of ice to be placed outside the ABC-TV studios at 44th Street in Times Square and a specially trained ice carver to create a space for him inside it. As the time approached, Blaine realized he might have second thoughts. He ordered his friend and the technical director for the event, William Kalush, "Don't pull me out under any circumstances between 10 and 11, preferably close to 11." He was referring to the live portion of the TV special.

On the morning of Monday, November 27, the ABC-TV show *Good Morning America* carried live the sealing of David Blaine into the block of ice. He entered shirtless and waving to the crowd that had gathered in Times Square to witness the event. He had with him a T-shirt, a knitted cap, and a photograph of his mother.

It wasn't long before he was frightened. "They seal it closed and I hear the noise of it sealing and I realize the ice is unbearably close, like an inch and a half away," he later told Joyce Wadler of the *New York Times*. "It's weird, I'm really terrified and freaking out. I think I'm not going to make it, I'm telling my guys to get me out." He had ordered them not to, however. Like it or not, he was in for the duration.

Unseasonably warm weather soon complicated the stunt. As the ice block began to melt, there was the chance that it could implode, or collapse in on itself. Blaine's crew piled bundles of dry ice on top of the block and used a special chemical compound to maintain the cube's shape. Blaine, who had put on the knitted stocking cap and T-shirt not long after he had been sealed into the cube, nodded and smiled at passersby, as he hopped from one foot to the other. This maneuver was not only to increase his body temperature but also to avoid standing motionless too long and enabling blood clots to form in his legs.

As the hours dragged by, Blaine found that although he had trained himself to sleep standing up, he was only able to doze briefly by leaning his stocking-capped head against the ice. Sleep deprivation was thus added to his other miseries. Around one-thirty that afternoon, it was discovered that someone had accidentally yanked on a tube leading to the catheter through which he relieved himself. Fortunately, it was repositioned.

As the time finally arrived for the ice to be cut away, Blaine was screaming. He managed to compose himself as he became visible to the cameras and the waiting crowd, but he was in bad shape, mumbling about having lost his mind. He was taken away on a stretcher and required a long recuperation.

He will never perform this stunt again, but he is not sorry he did it. "That's how I feel good," he says. Challenging himself with such feats is how he learns that he can "fight whatever they got." It's David Blaine against the world, a feeling he has had since he lost his mother.

At this writing, Blaine is developing a one-man stage show, to be produced by the Nederlander Organization in a warehouse in Manhattan's meat-packing district. "It's going to be simple and 'street'," he told *Time*. "It will have a story, not just a bunch of assembled tricks." At the turn of the twenty-first century, a magician of color actually had the choice to remain essentially a street magician.

Notes

1. Richard Potter:
The First American-born Magician

p. 8 Oliver Wendell Holmes poem excerpt . . . : *Negro Digest*, December 1949, p. 75.

p. 13 With his wife, Sally . . . : Milbourne Christopher, "Potter the Magician," *MUM* 43, no. 5 (October 1953): 177.

p. 14 Potter cried, "If you are not tolerant of spirits . . .": Jim Magus, *Magical Heroes: The Lives and Legends of Great African American Magicians* (Marietta, GA: Magus Entrprises, 1995), p. 24.

p. 16 The plot . . . : Gayraud S. Wilmore, *Black Religion and Black Radicalism: An Examination of the Black Experience in Religion* (Garden City, NY: Doubleday & Co., Inc., 1972), p. 65.

p. 17 "I am not just a colored man . . .": Magus, *Magical Heroes*, p. 25.

p. 17 "Mr. Potter will perform . . .": Ibid., p. 26.

p. 19 A Henry Hatton . . . : Christopher, "Potter the Magician," *MUM* p. 178.

p. 19 There is no record . . . : Diana Ross McCain, "A Nineteenth-Century Magician," *Early American Life* 26 (December 1995): 42.

p. 20 "Before a score . . .": Christopher, "Potter the Magician," p. 176.

2. Henry "Box" Brown:
An Escaped Slave Turned Magician

p. 28 Exchange between Brown and members of the Philadelphia Anti-Slavery Society: Henry Box Brown, *Narrative of the Life of Henry Box Brown, Written By Himself (1851)*, online version, University of North Carolina at Chapel Hill Libraries Documenting the American South project, p. 57.

p. 30 "For the next five minutes . . .": Magus, p. 50.

3. Minstrel Magicians

p. 39 "Son, if they hate me . . .": Robert C. Toll, "Behind the Black-face: Minstrel Men and Minstrel Myths," *American Heritage* 29 (April 1978): 105.

p. 42 "Everett the Magician . . .": Magus, *Magical Heroes*, p. 62.

p. 44 "A golden age . . .": Ibid., p. 64.

p. 45 "Without a doubt . . .": Ibid., p. 65.

p. 48 *Indianapolis Freeman* review: Henry T. Sampson, *The Ghost Walks: A Chronological History of Blacks in Show Business, 1865–1910* (Metuchen, NJ: Scarecrow Press, Inc., 1983), p. 361.

pp. 48–49 *Indianapolis Freeman* review: Magus, *Magical Heroes*, p. 67.

4. William Carl on the Vaudeville Stage

p. 54 Letter to *The Clipper*: Sampson, *Ghost Walks*, p. 187.

p. 55 *New Zealand Evening Post* review: Ibid., p. 186.

p. 56 *Pacific Commercial Advertiser* quotes: Ibid., pp. 203–205.

p. 57 "Yes, the popular demand . . .": Magus, *Magical Heroes*, p. 85.

p. 59 "The negroes are being overbearing . . .": James R. Grossman, *A Chance to Make Good: African Americans 1900–1929* (New York: Oxford University Press, 1999), p. 46.

p. 61 *Conjurer's Magazine* quote: Magus, *Magical Heroes*, p. 89.

5. The Refined Entertainment of the Celebrated Armstrongs

p. 63 ARMSTRONG RETURNED THE TRICK . . . : Magus, *Magical Heroes,* p. 108.
p. 65 "THE 1904 VAWTER . . .": David Price, *Magic: A Pictorial History of Conjurers in the Theater* (Cranbury, NJ: Cornwall Books, 1985), p. 392.
p. 66 "WE DID NOT REALIZE . . .": Ibid., p. 113.
p. 67 ADVERTISEMENT: Ibid., p. 114.

6. "Oriental" Conjurers

p. 84 "I BATHE . . .": "Fire Eater," *Ebony,* January 1953, p. 37.

7. Black Herman: "Once in Every Seven Years"

p. 93 HERMAN ON LIBERTY HALL PERFORMANCE: *The World's Greatest Magician: Black Herman* (Self-published, 1930s), pp. 37–38.
p. 94 "BEAUTIFUL PICTURES . . .": Ibid., p. 38.
p. 99 BLACK HERMAN PRESS RELEASES: Magus, *Magical Heroes,* p. 148.

8. Fetaque Sanders: From Discrimination to Equal Rights

p. 105 "SUPPOSE WE TRY ANOTHER TRICK . . .": Magus, *Magical Heroes,* p. 163.
p. 109 LETTER TO *THE NASHVILLE BANNER:* Maxine Thurman-Caruth, "Story Brought Back Some Magic Memories," *Nashville Banner,* October 9, 1991.
p. 110 "COLORED FOLKS . . .": Magus, *Magical Heroes,* p. 171.
p. 113 "I WORE OUT THREE TRAILERS . . .": Ibid., p. 186.
p. 115 "I DON'T DO TRICKS HERE . . .": Leon Alligood, "Past Has Been Magic for The Great Fetaque," *Nashville Banner,* September 17, 1991, p. B4.

9. Black Magicians in a Changing American Society

p. 119 Frank Brents publicity material: www.cs.yale.edu/homes/ mnm/bios.html.

p. 121 "In the past . . .": Barry Glassner, "Presto! It's Black Magic," *Sepia*, January 1977, p. 71.

p. 123 "That first show . . .": Ibid., p. 72.

p. 123 "A problem I have found . . .": Ibid., p. 73.

p. 124 "I'm happy to say . . .": "'Goldfinger' and Dove," *Ebony*, April 1977, p. 88.

p. 130 "Flash, originality . . .": Ibid., p. 90.

10. Today's Black Magicians

p. 135 "I have been lying . . ." and other Lemont Haskins quotes: From correspondence with Haskins, September–October 2000.

p. 135 He was once credited . . . . Magus, *Magical Heroes*, p. 199.

p. 146 "It may seem . . . ." correspondence with authors, May 1, 1998.

p. 146 "I'm being straight with you." Joyce Wadler, "A Latter-Day Houdini, Out of Cold Storage," *New York Times*, December 1, 2000, p. B2.

p. 149 "It's a roll of the dice. . . ." David Handelman, "The Wizard of Grunge," *Time*, May 19, 1997, p. 97.

p. 151 Balducci Levitation Solution: www.geocities.com/Broadway/Stage/7308/balducci.html.

p. 154 "Don't pull me out. . . . " Wadler, "A Latter-Day Houdini," p. B2.

p. 154 "They seal it closed. . . .": Ibid.

p. 155 "That's how I feel good." Ibid.

p. 155 "It's going to be simple and 'street' . . .". Handelman, "The Wizard of Grunge," p. 97.

Bibliography

Books

Brown, Henry Box. *Narrative of Henry Box Brown, Who Escaped from Slavery Enclosed in a Box 3 Feet Long and 2 Feet Wide*. Philadelphia.

Brown, Henry Box. *Narrative of the Life of Henry Box Brown, Written by Himself* (1851), online version University of North Carolina at Chapel Hill Libraries-Documenting the American South project http://docsouth.unc.edu/brownbox/brownbox.html.

Christopher, Milbourne, and Maureen Christopher. *The Illustrated History of Magic*. New York: Thomas Y. Crowell, 1973.

Fletcher, Tom. *100 Years of the Negro in Show Business!* New York: Burdge, 1954.

Grossman, James R. *A Chance to Make Good: African Americans 1900–1929*. New York: Oxford University Press, 1999.

Haskins, James. *Black Theater in America*. New York: Thomas Y. Crowell, 1982.

———. *Witchcraft, Mysticism and Magic in the Black World*. Garden City, NY: Doubleday and Company, Inc., 1974.

Haskins, Jim. *Get On Board: The Story of the Underground Railroad*. New York: Scholastic, 1993.

Herman, Black. *The World's Greatest Black Magician: Herman*. Self-published. New York, 1930s.

McKinley, Jesse. "High Temperatures Shrink Ice Man's Cocoon," *New York Times*, November 29, 2000, p. B-3.

Magus, Jim. *Magical Heroes: The Lives and Legends of Great African American Magicians*. Marietta, GA: Magus Enterprises, 1995.

Moulton, H. J. *Houdini's History of Magic in Boston, 1792–1915*. Glenwood, IL: Meyerbooks, 1983.

Price, David. *Magic: A Pictorial History of Conjurers in the Theater*. Cranbury, NJ: Cornwall Books, 1985.

Reed, Ishmael. *Mumbo Jumbo*. New York: Doubleday & Co., Inc., 1972.

Sampson, Henry T. *Blacks in Blackface: A Source Book on Early Black Musical Shows*. Metuchen, NJ: Scarecrow Press, Inc., 1980.

———. *The Ghost Walks: A Chronological History of Blacks in Show Business, 1865–1910*. Metuchen, NJ: Scarecrow Press, Inc., 1983.

Shine, Frances L. *Conjuror's Journal: Excerpts from the Journal of Joshua Medley*. New York: Dodd, Mead & Co., 1978.

Silverman, Kenneth. *Houdini: The Career of Erich Weiss*. New York: Harper Perennial, 1997.

The Success Book. Palo Alto, CA: Magic, Inc., 1973.

Wilmore, Gayraud S. *Black Religion and Black Radicalism: An Examination of the Black Experience in Religion*. Garden City, NY: Doubleday & Co., Inc., 1972.

ARTICLES

Alligood, Leon. "Past Has Been Magic for the Great Fetaque." *Nashville Banner*, September 17, 1991, pp. B-1+.

Carter, Rochelle. "With Every Magic Trick Was a Message." *The Tennessean*, June 6, 1992, p. B-5.

Christopher, Milbourne. "Potter the Magician." *MUM* 43, no. 5 (1953): 176–78.

"Escape Artist." *Ebony*, July 1957, pp. 67–68.

"Fire Eater." *Ebony*, January 1953, pp. 37+.

Glassner, Barry. "Presto! It's Black Magic." *Sepia*, January 1977, pp. 71–78.

"'Goldfinger' and Dove." *Ebony*, April 1977, pp. 88–90+.

Handelman, David. "The Wizard of Grunge." *Time*, May 19, 1997, p. 97.

Hunt, Gary. "Rannie in Boston." *Magical Past-Times: The On-Line Journal of Magic History*. www.velectric.com/pastimes/ranniead

Johnson, Helen A. "Blacks in Vaudeville: Broadway and Beyond." Conference on the History of American Popular Entertainment, New York Public Library at Lincoln Center, 1977. Westport, CT, 1979, pp. 77–86.

McCain, Diana Ross. "A Nineteenth-Century Magician." *Early American Life* 26 (1995): 42.

"Magic's Amazing Comeback." *Reader's Digest* 122, no. 732 (1983): 101–05.

"Miraculous Master of Magic." *Sepia*, July 1961, pp. 76–77.

"Rajah: The Magician." *Our World*, October 1949, pp. 52–55.

Ryan, James. "If He Can Conjure Magical Ratings, That's Some Trick." *New York Times*, May 11, 1997, pp. 43+.

Thurman-Caruth, Maxine. "Story Brought Back Some Magic Memories." *Nashville Banner*, October 9, 1991.

Toll, Robert C. "Behind the Blackface: Minstrel Men and Minstrel Myths." *American Heritage* 29 (1978): 93–105.

Wadler, Joyce. "A Latter-Day Houdini, Out of Cold Storage." *New York Times*, December 1, 2000, p. B-2.

Index